PRIVATE INTERNATIONAL LAW

PRIVATE INTERNATIONAL LAW

by

J. A. C. THOMAS

M.A., LL.B.

BARRISTER-AT-LAW; SENIOR LECTURER IN LAW IN THE UNIVERSITY OF GLASGOW

GREENWOOD PRESS, PUBLISHERS

WESTPORT, CONNECTICUT

Library of Congress Cataloging in Publication Data

Thomas, Joseph Anthony Charles.
Private international law.

Reprint of the 1955 ed. published by Hutchinson's University Library, London, in series: Hutchinson's university library: law.
Includes index.
1. Conflict of laws--Great Britain. I. Title.
[KD680.T46 1975] 340.9 74-31362
ISBN 0-8371-7929-7

Originally published in 1955 by Hutchinson's University Library, London

Reprinted with the permission of Hutchinson Publishing Group Ltd.

Reprinted in 1975 by Greenwood Press, a division of Williamhouse-Regency Inc.

Library of Congress Catalog Card Number 74-31362

ISBN 0-8371-7929-7

Printed in the United States of America

CONTENTS

PREFACE

THIS book aims to present an outline of the rules and principles of private international law in England. This, one of the younger offspring of the common law, is still developing relatively free from the mortifying influence of statute and there is, in consequence, ample room for controversy both over the proper formulation of existing principles and as to the desirable trends of future development. The views here expressed are those which to me seem most consistent with the present state of the authorities. If the book assists the prospective barrister or solicitor in preparing for his examinations, if it has some part in inducing the student reader to delve deeper into the subject, if it conveys to the general reader a picture of the problems of this branch of English law, I shall have achieved my object.

If, as I hope, the attempt to sketch within so small a compass a branch of the law which itself has ramifications throughout the field of legal relations has been not too rash a venture, it will have been in large measure due to the excellence of the literature on the subject and to the kindness of friends.

It would have been inappropriate to load this book with exhaustive footnotes and references. I would instead here acknowledge my indebtedness to such works as Dicey, *Conflict of Laws* (6th ed. 1949); Cheshire, *Private International Law* (4th ed. 1952); Graveson, *Conflict of Laws* (2nd ed. 1952); Schmitthoff, *English Conflict of Laws* (3rd ed. 1954).

My friends and former colleagues in the Department of Law of the University of Nottingham responded readily to my demands on their time and for their opinions while the book was in progress. Mr. G. Hibbard, M.A., of the Department of English in the same University, read the manuscript and gave me much valuable advice. Professor O. Kahn-Freund, Ll.M., Dr. Jur., of the Law Department of the London School of Economics, read the book in manuscript and there are few places in which I have not profited from the helpful criticisms and suggestions of his great learning. To all I would express my sincere gratitude. For the defects which remain I am alone responsible.

J. A. C. T.

Glasgow.
11th February, 1955.

TABLE OF CASES

TABLE OF STATUTES

GLOSSARY OF LATIN TERMS USED

Bona vacantia	Residuary estate upon an intestacy when the deceased dies without any relatives or other persons legally entitled to claim the property.
Dicta	Judicial statements of law which are not essential elements in the decision arrived at by the court.
Forum	Court: place where an action is brought.
In personam	(Lit.) Against a person. An action *in personam* is one in which relief by way of damages, injunction, or specific performance is sought against a particular person or group of persons.
In rem	(Lit.) Against a thing. An action *in rem* is one affecting the title to property.
Inter vivos	Between living persons.
Lex actus	The law governing an act or transaction.
Lex causae	The system of law by which the rights of the parties to an action are to be determined.
Lex domicilii	The law of the place of one's domicile.
Lex fori	The law of the place before whose courts an action is brought.
Lex loci actus	The law of the place where an act is done or a transaction effected.
Lex loci celebrationis	The law of the place where a marriage is celebrated.
Lex loci contractus	The law of the place where a contract is made.

Lex loci delicti . . .	The law of the place where a wrong is committed.
Lex loci solutionis . .	The law of the place where a contractual obligation is to be performed.
Lex patriae . . .	The law of one's nationality.
Lex situs (*or Lex rei sitae*)	The law of the place where property is situate.
Lex successionis . .	The law governing a succession.
Locus regit actum . .	The validity of an act or transaction is governed by the law of the place where it takes place.
Mobilia personam sequuntur	Movables follow the person of their owner: i.e., the personal law of the owner determines the effect of dispositions and transactions affecting property.
Per subsequens matrimonium	By subsequent marriage.
Situs	The place where property is situate.

CHAPTER ONE

INTRODUCTION AND GENERAL PRINCIPLES

A. NATURE AND PURPOSE OF RULES OF PRIVATE INTERNATIONAL LAW

CASES frequently arise before an English court, whose facts are not exclusively connected with England. There may be, for instance, a dispute over a contract made between a Frenchman and an Englishman in Brussels for the delivery of goods from Paris to London; or a petition by a woman for a divorce from her husband whose home is in France; or a claim by a Spaniard against an Italian who negligently ran him down with a motor-car in Oxford. The common feature of all these examples is the existence of relevant facts which may make it necessary for the court to do more than merely refer to the provisions of English law.

In any such case, in fact, the court has at least two questions to answer before it can determine the rights of the parties:

(i) has it jurisdiction to entertain the claim?

In the divorce example, above, for instance, is the English court competent to hear the petition or must it tell the woman to seek relief in France?

(ii) (assuming that it has jurisdiction) what is the system of law by which the rights of the parties are to be determined?

In other words, is the court to apply the ordinary rules of English law or, using the same example, should it apply French divorce law?

The answer to each question is found by the application of the English rules of Private International Law.

The number of separate systems of law in the world, differing among themselves in their treatment of contract, property, matrimonial questions, etc., makes it essential that the courts of each system should have some guide to determine whether they may deal with a case which has links with another system, and whether they should apply their own law or not. It would, of course, be perfectly possible for courts simply to apply in all cases the ordinary principles which obtain in cases unaffected by a foreign element. That, however, would mean that the rights of the parties could be affected by the fortuitous selection of one set of courts rather than another for their litigation. The outcome of the action might depend, for example, on whether the parties had their dispute decided in England rather than in France. The mutual respect due between states and practical considerations of expediency, no less than the sense of justice, militate against such an approach.

Hence all systems of law have evolved rules and principles to assist them in determining the scope of their own jurisdiction and the selection of the appropriate governing law in a case with foreign connections. This book is concerned with those adopted in the courts of England and which are here styled 'Private International Law'. That name has not escaped criticism. In truth, no satisfactory title for the subject has yet been proposed. 'Conflict of Laws' is an alternative which has much support; but Private International Law is much used and the practical inconvenience of introducing yet another alternative is sufficient justification for its retention here.

Though all systems of law may have rules for dealing with 'foreign element' cases, they do not all have the same rules. For instance, English courts turn to the law of the domicile of the person concerned (*lex domicilii*) in matters of personal status, while most continental systems of law look to the law of the person's nationality (*lex patriae*): in like manner, the rules relating to contract, civil injuries, etc., vary from state to state. It follows that cases may still be decided differently according as they are brought in the courts of one state rather than those of another, a result which it is really the object of private international law to prevent.

Frequent efforts have been made to eliminate this inconvenience—indeed, reproach—by international conferences and conventions aimed at the introduction of uniform rules in all states on a given topic. Some of these attempts have met with a large measure of success as, for instance, the Berne Convention of 1886 on copyright and the Warsaw Convention 1929 on air traffic which were given effect in England by the International Copyright Act 1886 and the Carriage by Air Act 1932 respectively. On the other hand, numerous conventions at The Hague and

Geneva on such important topics as marriage laws, guardianship, etc., have secured only varying (and generally small) numbers of adherents: to none has Great Britain subscribed. The record, then, of attempts at international co-operation in this field to date is scarcely encouraging. At the same time, any efforts to ensure that private international law does fulfil its object of securing uniformity of result in a given sphere deserve the strongest support.

It remains to mention that, for the purposes of private international law, all legal systems other than English are foreign: a case with Scottish or Northern Irish connections would thus be a case with foreign elements in an English court.

B. Historical Outline

The rules of private international law now in use have, in the main, been the product of a long historical development which merits some consideration. The story of private international law really began in the twelfth century in Italy, as a by-product of the revival in Roman Law studies. By that time, distinct countries and states were re-arising in Europe after the confusion of the so-called Dark Ages and scholars were turning to the compilation of Roman Law by the Emperor Justinian (A.D. 527–565) as a kind of legal *lingua franca* of the Western world. Justinian's Code commences with an ordinance addressed to 'all peoples who are subject to our clement sway';[1] in other words, it is addressed in terms to Roman subjects only. This was used to justify the proposition that a sovereign's laws govern only his own subjects—just as Justinian could lay down laws only for the Romans, so a modern ruler could regulate by his rules and decrees only his own subjects. This meant that systems of law had each a limited application and so stimulated an inquiry into the sphere of operation of systems of law.

The first fruit of this investigation was a distinction between matters of substance and matters of procedure; that is to say, between questions as to the actual rights and duties of the parties and questions as to the machinery of justice invoked to determine those rights and duties. Substance, it was held, depended upon the *lex loci actus*, i.e., the law of the place where the transaction

[1] Cod. I. 1. 1.: generally called '*Cunctos Populos*', from the first words of the Latin text.

was effected, from which the rights and duties arose: for, when they entered upon their transaction, the parties were subjects of the ruler of that place because they were present in his realm. Procedure was to be governed by the *lex fori*, the law of the place whose courts were invoked; for it is the ruler whose courts they are who may say how those courts are to operate.

Pursuing the inquiry further, there came the Theory of Statutes in fourteenth-century Italy. Granted the limited applicability of rules of law, the question was to know when a given rule should be applicable. This, said the Statutists, was to be determined by the nature of the rule itself. Rules (or statutes) might be real, personal or mixed, according as they concerned property, persons or both. Real and mixed statutes would be wholly local in their operation so that, for instance, a rule of state X concerning the disposition of land would be operative in respect of all land in state X, no matter where the disposition was effected—if one wished to conclude a sale in state Y of a piece of land in X, one would have to comply with the appropriate laws of X. Personal laws of a sovereign, however, governed his subjects wherever they might be. Hence, if the question at issue was the personal capacity, say, of a contracting party, then the matter would be governed by his *lex domicilii*, the law of the place of his permanent home, no matter where the contract was made or its subject-matter situated. The whole basis of this approach was, in fact, very faulty; for it may be virtually impossible to say confidently that a given rule is real or otherwise. Nevertheless, great advances were made. For instance, in the field of contract, Bartolus (1314–57) suggested that, by reason of the complexity of the matter, subdivisions should be made—the formation of the contract should be governed by the *lex loci contractus*, its performance by the *lex loci solutionis*. A French successor, Dumoulin (1500–66), urged that rather should the law chosen by the parties determine the question of contract. Similar developments were made in other spheres of juridical activity.

Statutism held the field until the rise of the Dutch School of jurists in the seventeenth century. As was perhaps natural in a newly independent state, these jurists—the greatest of whom was Huber (1636–94)—stressed the control of the local ruler over what happens in his courts. It followed that the application of foreign law in a case depends upon the permission of the local sovereign, a permission which is forthcoming because of the comity which exists between nations. This teaching is important because it observes that the rules evolved under Statutism (e.g., that the *lex domicilii* governs capacity to contract) are not universal verities with a validity deriving, as it were, from their inner selves. In so far as they may be adopted by the courts of any legal system, they are rules of that system, which could have framed others for itself but which has found it convenient to adopt those already in existence.

As new states emerged and old states acquired new forms of government, subsequent developments on the continent after the impact of the Dutch have been characterized, broadly speaking, by the manifestation of nationalism in the principles adopted for matters involving foreign elements. The lead in this trend was given by the French. National pride in the Revolution is reflected in the French Code which adopted nationality as the test of personal status and gave the courts of France sweeping jurisdiction over suits involving Frenchmen. Similarly, in Italy, the departure of foreign rulers and the unification of the nation resulted in the adoption of nationality as the basis of private law questions. Such developments were possible as a result of the teachings of the Dutch. It was for the local sovereign to indicate the principles on which jurisdiction would be taken and the circumstances in which the application of foreign law in his courts would be entertained.

Continental developments have been considered because the early history of private international law in England was much influenced by them, especially by the Dutch. For the retarded development of this branch of English law, there are various reasons. Through the early unification of the common law, which already prevailed throughout the realm by the fourteenth century, England encountered none of the difficulties in her island which beset the numerous little states of medieval Europe. Again, the requirement that juries should be drawn from the district where the facts arose prevented the courts from taking jurisdiction over questions arising abroad. But by the eighteenth century the jury rule had been relaxed, while the growth of the empire brought an acquaintance with other systems of law in countries now under British rule. Moreover, the incorporation of commercial law (hitherto regarded as a kind of international custom extraneous to the common law) into the common law of England by Lord Mansfield (1705–93) squarely raised the need to deal with foreign element cases, as our commercial prosperity grew. In such circumstances, the foreign authorities were freely drawn upon for assistance in dealing with this new type of problem. A further, if indirect, source of continental influence came through the work of the American, Story, in the early part of last century. As the first important writer in English on this topic, and a distinguished representative of a legal system close to that of England, Story naturally exercised a powerful influence in the English courts; and Story had borrowed from the continent.

English literature on this branch of the law has a very short history. Dicey's important treatise first appeared only in 1896 and, with re-editing, is still the leading English work. But since Dicey the literature has flourished and continues to expand. This is a matter of importance for, by reason of the comparatively late development of English private international law, there are still many *lacunae* and doubts, so that writings play a greater part here than is customary in the formulation of the law in England.

C. Classification and Renvoi

In the course of the long history of this topic from the twelfth century, there have been evolved various rules for different situations, to assist the courts to determine whether they have jurisdiction and to what legal system they should look for the principles to decide the point at issue in a foreign element case. Examples are the rules: Capacity to marry is governed by the *lex domicilii* of the person in question: Title to land is determined by the *lex situs*: Procedure is governed by the *lex fori*, etc. The first task for a court, therefore, when seized of a foreign element case is to invoke the appropriate rule. But that in itself involves the determination of the legal category to which the problem before the court belongs. The court has to decide, for instance, that the legal question involved on the facts before it is one of capacity to marry in order to select the relevant rule. This is the process known as classification.

Every rule of private international law has two parts, usually styled respectively the 'operative facts' and the 'connecting factor'. The former designates the type of problem raised, the latter is a guide to the system by whose rules its solution is to be found. Thus, in the capacity rule cited above, capacity to marry is the operative fact; domicile is the connecting factor. Suppose that a woman seeks a decree of the nullity of her marriage in England on the ground that, by the law of Utopia, where she was married, persons under twenty-one cannot legally marry, and she was only twenty at the time of the ceremony. The problem raised is clearly, Was she able to marry?, i.e., a question of capacity. Applying the rule, the court will ascertain where she was domiciled at the time of her purported marriage and determine the suit by reference to the rules of her *lex domicilii* concerning capacity to marry. Only if she were domiciled in Utopia, will the Utopian rule be relevant as such: if she were domiciled in Arcadia, then the Arcadian rule on capacity will be decisive.

In so ascertaining the question under consideration, it may be necessary to classify a legal rule or principle relied upon by one of the parties. Suppose that it is established that the question before the court is one of capacity to marry, that the woman was domiciled in Utopia at the time of the ceremony and that the full rule of Utopian law is that a person under twenty-one must have his or her parent's consent to marry. The court has to decide whether that is in truth a rule relating to capacity. Does it mean that there is no ability at all to marry without such consent? Or does it mean that a person under twenty-one may marry but must first observe the formality of asking parental consent? If the former interpretation be correct, the marriage would be void; if the second meaning be the true one, then the Utopian provision would relate not to capacity but to the formalities of the marriage and would have no bearing upon the question before the court.

Where rules of law fall to be classified, difficulties may arise because the rule in question may be one which is not known as such in English law itself. In such case, the court will obviously have to find some category to which the foreign principle is analogous and for which a private international law rule does exist. For simply to say that, because the problem was unfamiliar, no remedy could be given here would be woeful weakness. It would indeed be possible for the court to accept a new legal category and frame a new rule accordingly, but legal conservatism would make that an unlikely eventuality. The quest for an analogy would thus be the probable course.

Since the success of classification in dealing with such problems will depend upon the breadth of view taken in finding analogies, much has been written on the manner in which classification should be approached. The value of the literature is, however, somewhat doubtful, for the court's classification of the question before it will invariably proceed by an apparently natural absorption of that question within some category. It has to be remembered that the parties will have pleaded their respective cases, setting out their claims and the arguments and evidence on which they rely; in these circumstances, the court is usually able, without expressly adverting to the point, to find that the problem is one of capacity to marry, of succession to landed property, etc. It is indeed significant that discussion of the question of classification does not figure largely in the law reports in England: but that does not mean that English courts have never had to classify.

Certain factors which it is desirable that courts should bear in mind—and which appear to be exemplified by the authorities—may be stressed. In the first place, fully to appreciate the true effect of a foreign rule raised before it, the court should consider the operation of that rule within its own legal system: it could be misleading to consider, say, a rule of French law in the abstract without any reference to the general picture of that branch of French law to which the rule belongs. Again, when seeking an analogy for the rule whose operation is so ascertained, the court should be generous in interpreting its own legal categories and concepts, so making easier the task of accommodating the foreign rule. These points may be illustrated by reference to decided instances of good classification.

In *Huntington v. Attrill*,[1] the facts were that a New York statute provided that company directors should be personally liable for the debts of the company where false reports of its financial situation had been published, sums so chargeable being

[1] [1893] A.C. 150

recoverable by the creditors. A creditor sued under this statute in New York and got judgment for a large sum, which he now sought to enforce in Ontario where the defendant, a director of the company, was living. It is, in English law, a principle of public policy that foreign penal judgments will not be enforceable in England and the law of Ontario has a similar rule. It was shown that in New York the provisions of the statute in question were regarded as penal, but the Privy Council, sitting as a court of appeal from Ontario, nevertheless held that the judgment could be enforced in that province.

Their Lordships held that it was for the Ontario courts themselves to decide whether the statute was penal: as it operated in New York to give damages to persons who were misled by false reports, it was—by Ontarian standards—remedial, not penal, i.e., not directed principally to the punishment of the wrongdoer. This helpful decision emphasizes that

(a) the operation of the foreign provision must be studied, as it were, 'in its native surroundings'
(b) classification is a matter of fitting the *foreign* problem into the appropriate pigeonhole in the *municipal* legal categories.

Again, in *De Nicols v. Curlier*,[1] a man and woman, both resident and domiciled in France, had married there without making a marriage contract to determine the distribution of their marital property. The consequence, in French law, would be that their estate became subject to 'community of goods' whereby each acquired a half-share in all property acquired by either during the currency of the marriage. They later became domiciled in England and started in London a café which prospered and became the Café Royal. At the husband's death, some £600,000 stood to his name and his will purported to dispose of the whole. The widow now claimed that, by reason of French law, she was absolutely entitled to half that sum, so that the will could affect only the other half. The House of Lords accepted that contention.

The relevant rule of English private international law is: Property relations of spouses are governed

(a) if there be no marriage contract, by the *lex domicilii* for the time being

[1] [1900] A.C. 21

(b) if there be a marriage contract, by its 'proper law', the law which the parties intended to govern their contract.

It was thus necessary to classify the French rule which had no English counterpart. If it operated as a contract, the widow would succeed; if it did not, then English law as the *lex domicilii* would determine the claim. Their Lordships, being satisfied that in France community of goods applied automatically in the absence of an express contract, held that the French rule was really in the nature of an implied contract between the spouses and so governed their property rights despite their change of domicile to England. This decision from our highest court again emphasizes the need to consider a foreign rule in its proper setting and not to take too narrow a view of the municipal concepts in seeking a pigeon-hole for the foreign provision.

The object of classification, as said, is to invoke the appropriate rule for selecting the system by which the legal problem before the court is to be determined. In general, that selection is of the municipal law of the system referred to. If, for instance, French law is the appropriate law, then the rules thereof are applied which would apply in France in a purely French case.

There are, however, certain cases in which some foreign systems of law adopt a different approach and look not merely to the municipal law of the chosen system but to its rules of private international law and, guided by them, select the rules to determine the issue. For instance, in *Forgo's Case*,[1] F, a Bavarian national, died intestate, domiciled in France; by French private international law, the French court was referred to Bavarian law, F's *lex patriae*, as governing his succession. The Bavarian rule for intestate succession, however, referred to the *lex domicilii* of a deceased person, here French law. The French court accepted this direction from the Bavarian rule and proceeded to determine the disposition of F's estate by the internal law of France. This process is known as *renvoi* and operates where the law of the *forum* uses a different connecting factor from the law governing the issue (*lex causae*). The object, it will be seen, is to ensure that the *forum* gives the same decision which would have been given, had the issue come before the courts of the legal system which governs it. In the *Forgo* case, for instance, because, in the courts

[1] Clunet 1883, p. 64

of Bavaria, French law would have been applied to determine the succession, the French court before which the case in fact came applied French law, so ensuring that the decision would conform with the view of F's national courts.

This acceptance of redirection from the private international law of another system is not, as such, adopted in English courts. But in some cases where the relevant foreign system does adopt this *renvoi*, an English court, referred to that system, will give effect to the *renvoi* by an elaborate process known as 'Double' or 'Foreign Court' *renvoi*.

In these cases, the English court, being referred to, say, French law, then considers itself to be a French court and views the facts before it afresh as if it were a case arising in a French court. The judge, as it were, ceases to be an English judge and becomes a French judge dealing with the facts. Accordingly, he has then to adopt the relevant French private international law practice and thus, if necessary, *renvoi*. Let us assume that the case involves an Englishman and that, since French law does observe the practice of *renvoi*, the judge accordingly finds himself referred by the French private international rule to English law, including private international practice. Since *renvoi* is not part of English practice, he finds that English rules direct him to French municipal law to provide a solution of the problem. The position, therefore, is that the judge, having originally turned to French law in accord with English private international law, is referred back by French law to English private international law; but that body of rules still directs him to apply French law. The question he now has to answer is, Does French law accept this reference back from English law? If it does, then he will now—as it were, at the second attempt—apply French municipal law: if, as in Italy, the reference back would not be accepted, then the court will apply the relevant provision of English municipal law—but selected by the private international law of France. In short, on reference to French law in the first place, the court notionally becomes a French court; everything that happens thereafter is determined as it would be in France.

A concrete example will illustrate this complicated manoeuvre. In *Re Annesley*,[1] an Englishwoman died domiciled in France,

[1] [1926] Ch. 692

leaving a will which was valid by the internal law of England but not by that of France. The question was, Is the will valid? Russell J. finding that the problem, as one of succession, fell to French law as the woman's *lex domicilii*, then regarded himself as a French judge charged with deciding the case. As the French succession rule referred to the *lex patriae*, of the deceased, he then found himself directed to regard the facts of the case as an English court would view them—and so found himself redirected to apply French law. The question now was, Could he, as a French judge, apply French municipal law on the direction of the English rule (which, of course, was notionally a foreign rule to him)? Being satisfied that French law did accept the *renvoi*, he held that he could so apply French law; thus he finally reached the conclusion that the will was not valid because it did not comply with French municipal law.

As stated, the number of instances in which English courts adopt this procedure is limited. It is found only in questions concerning succession to property on death and, apparently, in determining personal status.[1]

Much academic criticism has been levelled, mainly on logical grounds, against 'double *renvoi*'. It is, however, thought that, though the process may be mechanically clumsy, it is an attempt to solve a practical difficulty. The cases in which it is employed are cases where unanimity of result is pre-eminently desirable, but in which the common law and continental systems use different connecting factors—domicile and nationality respectively. If an English court were to apply forthwith the municipal law of the system to which it is referred as the *lex domicilii*, it might reach a different result from that which would be reached by the courts of the domicile, which would have referred to the *lex patriae*. Yet it is agreed that, for English purposes, the domiciliary law should govern the disposition of the estate or the determination of the status problem. It is therefore reasonable that the English court should endeavour to give the same decision that the courts of the domicile would give.

The chief difficulty raised by 'double *renvoi*'—like all the others, more theoretical than practical—is that there is, strictly speaking, no such thing as British law nor yet an English nation-

[1] cf. *Re Askew* [1930] 2 Ch. 259

ality.[1] British nationality covers persons living subject to a variety of legal systems—English, Scots, Roman-Dutch, etc. Hence, when referred back to the *lex patriae* in the case of an Englishman who dies domiciled in, say, Italy, which does not accept a *renvoi*, an English court is forced into a technical impossibility. That difficulty has, however, been met—practically, if in a manner objectionable to the purist—by construing the reference to the *lex patriae* as a reference to the law of that part of the United Kingdom from which the deceased hailed. In the same way, a Jamaican's *lex patriae*, for these purposes, would be the law of Jamaica.

At the same time, the patent artifice of the process is itself an argument against unnecessary extension of the 'double *renvoi*' procedure. It is therefore stressed that, save in the very few cases specified, a reference to a foreign system by English private international law is a reference to the municipal law of that system. There may indeed be hope that, in time, the need for its use will be entirely removed by the elimination of *renvoi* in general. A Convention at The Hague in 1951, to which Great Britain was a party, would, if universally adopted, go far to achieve this effect. For its first Article provides that, where the circumstances exist in which double *renvoi* is at present practised, the municipal law of the *lex domicilii* shall be applied.

D. Proof of Foreign Law

Before the question whether foreign law is applicable can arise at all—with its consequent problems of classification and the interpretation of the relevant foreign provisions—the parties must have raised the issue. It is not for the judge to suggest that a foreign system of law might be appropriate in a case before him. He is an English judge in an English court, sworn to administer English law, and, indeed, English law is the only system of which knowledge can be imputed to him. In consequence, foreign law, if the parties wish to raise it, must be proved to him: it is a matter of fact, and, like other facts, must be established by evidence.

[1] Under the British Nationality Act 1948, each member of the Commonwealth may regulate its own citizenship, the residuary citizenship being that of the United Kingdom and Colonies: these developments, however, do not affect the problem here under discussion.

Of course, the parties may be agreed as to the substance and effect of the relevant foreign rules and thus submit an agreed statement thereof to the court. In such circumstances, the legal provisions in question would be admitted facts and, as such, would require no further proof. But, more often, parties are in conflict over the applicable foreign law and, in such case, they must call evidence to establish their respective assertions and the court will have to decide which is the true position.

It is for the English court to determine the competence of witnesses as to foreign law no less than that of witnesses to fact proper. In this matter, English courts have always preferred the evidence of persons with a practical knowledge of the legal system in question. The views of, say, an ordinary French layman as to the French law of succession would not be acceptable, any more than those of an English layman on some topic of English law could be relied on. More particularly, one may say, the courts want the evidence of persons who are either practitioners of the particular legal system or whose normal occupation necessitates their having a practical acquaintance of that system. That is the type of expert witness that the parties must call. Thus, in a case where the French law of contract was in issue, a mere student of French law in, say, an English university would not be eligible, when there is available a French judge or barrister or even perhaps the secretary of a French commercial company. In *De Béeche v. South American Stores*,[1] indeed, the court relied upon the evidence of a London banker, who had had experience of banking in South America, to ascertain the effect of a bill of exchange made in Chile.

If, as not infrequently happens, the expert witnesses on either side disagree in their views, then of course the court has to resolve this clash of evidence. The manner in which this is done cannot be categorically stated. It may be that the court will prefer the opinion of one expert to that of the other. On the other hand, the court may reject all the evidence and construe the foreign law for itself, as did Wynn Parry J. in *Re Duke of Wellington*,[2] when the experts revealed themselves in conflict on the question whether Spanish law accepted a reference back from the relevant

[1] [1935] A.C. 148
[2] [1947] Ch. 506

foreign legal system in its application of the doctrine of *renvoi.*

It may be that a party pleads the applicability of foreign law to determine his claim, but fails to produce any evidence of the law in question. In such case the judge is bound to apply English law to decide the case even though it be apparent that, by the rules of private international law, English law is not really the proper law of the dispute. In the absence of evidence, there is a presumption that the content of a foreign system of law is the same as that of English law. Only in the case of one tribunal may the court take cognizance of another system of law without proof: the House of Lords, being the ultimate court of appeal not only for England but also for Scotland and Northern Ireland, needs no proof of the content of Scots and Northern Ireland law.

The simplest method of obtaining knowledge of the law of another state upon a given point would seem to be to obtain a ruling of the courts of that state upon the point; though possibly productive of delay and expense, it would ensure accuracy. Statutory provision for the adoption of this course was in fact made in the mid-nineteenth century. The British Law Ascertainment Act 1859 authorizes a court in any British territory to send a case to a court in any other such territory for the opinion of that court on the law applicable to the facts in the case so sent: a similar provision in respect of sending cases to courts of countries foreign, in the customary sense of the word, is made by the Foreign Law Ascertainment Act 1861. For some reason, however, the procedure under these Acts seems to have been always viewed with disfavour; at least, its use has been rare.

E. Exclusion of Foreign Law

The discussion has hitherto concerned the selection and meaning of 'foreign law' in the application of private international rules. There are, however, some circumstances in which, though the case would, on normal principles, be governed by some foreign system—under which it would present enforceable rights and duties—the particular features of the facts before the court require that the normal rules should not prevail. This occurs when, in the opinion of the court, it would be contrary to the policy of its own state to recognize legal consequences as flowing from the situation before it.

The principle is an old, and also essentially a sound, one. As an English judge once said, "It seems to me almost absurd to suppose that the Courts of this country should enforce a contract which they consider to be against public policy simply because it happens to be made somewhere else."[1] At the same time, if the conscience of the *forum* be hypersensitive, there is a great danger that the ends of private international law would be defeated. For, if the appropriate foreign law be excluded, it follows that the facts before the court are subjected to the *lex fori*: and excessive application of the *lex fori* would obviously be the negation of recognition of rights regulated by a foreign legal system. In England, the exercise of this excluding power is—as it must be—discretionary; but it is not arbitrary. There are some well-defined circumstances in which, on this ground, claims will not be enforced in English courts; for the rest, normal principles prevail.

Thus, a foreign penal judgment will not be enforced in England nor will a claim for foreign taxes: English courts are not gaolers or debt-collecting agencies for other states. On similar principles, English courts would refuse to enforce a foreign decree purporting to confiscate property of its nationals. In like manner, our courts would deny remedies in respect of transactions which offend against basic ideas of English morality. Hence, in *Hope v. Hope*,[2] the court would not enforce a contract whereby a husband had agreed to pay his wife an allowance if she facilitated divorce proceedings, because it was tainted with collusion. Similarly, in *Kaufman v. Gerson*,[3] action would not lie in England on a contract, governed and valid by French law, because, by English standards, it savoured of 'blackmail'. Nor will the court enforce in England provisions which are inconsistent with the freedom of person and action of the individual, even though they be provisions of his *lex domicilii*: a man may be a slave in his own country but he may not be treated as one in England.

In this connection, it is necessary to distinguish between a status and its 'incidents', as they are usually termed. Status may

[1] *Rousillon v. Rousillon* (1880) 14 Ch.D. 351, 369 per Fry J.
[2] (1857) 8 De G.M. & G. 731
[3] [1904] 1 K.B. 591

be defined as the state of possessing certain legal capacities and/or incapacities—those capacities and incapacities are its incidents. For instance, in English law, an infant (a person under twenty-one) is said to have a status because he has only a limited power to make contracts, no power to be the legal owner of land, etc. In the same way, all persons have, in the field of private international law, a status; and the determination thereof and the extent of its incidents are matters for the *lex domicilii.*

Now his *lex domicilii* may impose a status upon a person which subjects him to disabilities, such as England would consider derogatory to human dignity: an obvious example is the slave of former days, a human being treated as a chattel with no legal rights. In such cases, it is the doctrine of English law that the status given by the domicile will be recognized but its incidents will not necessarily be enforced in England. In *Sommersett's Case,*[1] for example, the owner of a West Indian slave was not allowed to recover him as piece of property in England when the slave escaped from his hands. Again, in *Worms v. De Valdor,*[2] the court ignored a restriction imposed upon the freedom of a Frenchman, adjudged a prodigal in France, to deal in financial matters: that a grown man should be prevented from conducting his own business affairs did not accord with English notions of adult independence.

It is, perhaps, in such circumstances, that the dangers of the excluding power of public policy can best be seen. While in a civilized society slavery would indeed be reprobated, it is surely questionable whether an attempt to prevent a spendthrift from frittering away his property should be regarded as reprehensible. In any status matters, it is to be feared, public policy has a detrimental effect. Rightly or wrongly, there are states, for instance, in which interracial marriages are forbidden—should a white and a negro, both domiciled in Louisiana where such a restriction prevails, be free to marry in England, the ban being ignored as being against English public policy? It would be a pointless display of English tolerance, if the parties remained domiciled in Louisiana. To consider another example, an order for the maintenance of a child, made in the domicile of the

[1] (1772) 20 St. Tr. 1
[2] (1880) 49 L.J. Ch. 261

parent concerned, may yet be given no effect in England on the ground of public policy, because it imposes a greater liability than could an English order of a similar type. In such case, English notions of public policy would work undoubted injustice. In fairness, it must be said that such dangers are not peculiar to England alone but are inherent in the application of the public policy principle in all systems.

Such considerations give added importance to the limitations upon the scope of public policy. It operates only where there is sought in England actual enforcement of an offending provision: it will not prevent recognition of the effective operation of the offending provision in the place of its origin. As seen in *Sommersett's Case*, a slave could not be kept as a chattel in England: but, in *Santos v. Illidge*,[1] an English court recognized the validity of a sale of slaves made in Brazil, where slavery was at the time lawful, and, indeed, allowed a claim for the price of the unhappy creatures. The buyer had received in Brazil something which was treated as property in that country and must pay for what he bought. The English court was not required to turn the slaves into chattels; they had already been so degraded in Brazil and the court here could but recognize the fact. Again, polygamy is against public policy—no polygamous marriage could be contracted in England and no English matrimonial relief would be given to a polygamously married person. But that does not prevent an English court from recognizing as married a Hindu who has married in India by polygamous Hindu rites.[2] The fact that a Hindu ceremony in England would not create a valid marriage does not prevent recognition of its having done so in India.

F. General Principles of English Jurisdiction

From general consideration of the question of the application of foreign law, we turn to the circumstances in which English courts will accept jurisdiction over cases involving a foreign element. As the Dutch observed, a territorial sovereign can effectively control only those who are his subjects, whether by birth or by presence temporarily within his domain: but it is

[1] (1860) 8 C.B.N.S. 861
[2] *Baindail v. Baindail* [1946] P. 122

possible for others to submit their disputes to his adjudication. That approach is reflected in the common law principles of English jurisdiction which are based respectively upon Effectiveness and Submission.

(i) Effectiveness

In personal actions or actions *in personam*, as they are called, i.e., those to recover a debt, damages, etc., it is necessary that the defendant be present in England at the time that proceedings are commenced against him; that is to say, he must be capable of being served with due process of the law. Basically, this is sound: if the man is in England, then he can be brought before the court and subjected to its judgment. The principle in some circumstances, however, may be observed only in the most formal sense. The crucial time is, in general, that of the commencement of proceedings, the issue of the writ. So long as the defendant is then in England, the court will have effective jurisdiction over him, although, by the time that the case comes to trial, he may well have left England and not set foot again in this country.

Actions *in rem*, those which seek to affect the title to property, can, in general, be entertained in England only if the property be situate in England; only in such circumstances would an English judgment be effective. Similarly, the underlying principle of English divorce jurisdiction is that only persons domiciled in England may petition here for divorce. Since the dissolution of a marriage is the termination of the marital status, it should be exclusively within the competence of the domicile of the parties to the marriage. However, many inroads have now been made upon that basic principle and the whole topic of matrimonial jurisdiction will be more fully considered in Chapter Two.

(ii) Submission

This is a ground of jurisdiction in personal claims and, as its name suggests, signifies that the parties—more particularly the defendant—concede the competence of the court to deal with their dispute, even though the defendant is not in England at any time during the course of the action.

Such submission may be express, as, for instance, when it is provided in a contract that any dispute arising out of the contract shall be determined by the English courts. It may also be implied from the conduct of the parties, where, for example, the defendant, having been served with notice of the English proceedings against him, defends the action on its merits without taking the point that the court is not entitled to assume jurisdiction: *Boyle v. Sacker*.[1]

Such are the circumstances in which an action may be validly commenced at common law in England. It was felt, however, that these requirements were too limiting. If, for instance, the defendant, a Frenchman, were no longer in England, then a person who had been injured by him in London would be unable to obtain redress from him in an English court, although the scene of the accident and all the witnesses were in this country.

In consequence, from the Common Law Procedure Act 1852 onwards, statutory extensions of English jurisdiction were made. These provisions are now comprised in Order XI of the Rules of the Supreme Court and have the appearance of going almost to the other extreme in providing a wide range of situations in which application may be made to the Court for permission to bring an action in England against a person who is outside England. For example, the fact that a contract was made in England authorizes such an application, although the parties may be foreigners, the contract was to be performed, and the breach, out of which the dispute arises, occurred in another country.[2] The granting of such applications is, however, in the discretion of the court and it is in the careful exercise of their discretion by the judges that the foreign defendant has his greatest protection from abuse of Order XI procedure.

The courts further claim the power to order the staying of either action in cases where proceedings are taken in both England and some other state in respect of the same subject-matter. This jurisdiction, though asserted, is most carefully exercised and instances are rare. For the courts are fully conscious of the possibility of very real advantages being obtainable from each set of proceedings; as may be seen from the discussions in *McHenry v. Lewis*[3] and *Cohen v. Rothfield*.[4]

[1] (1888) 39 Ch.D. 249
[2] R.S.C. Order XI, r.1 (e) (i)
[3] (1882) 22 Ch.D. 397
[4] [1919] 1 K.B. 410

G. Domicile

Domicile is properly considered among the general principles in that matters of personal status arise in so many branches of the law and such questions are referred, in English private international law, to the *lex domicilii.* It has been already observed that many continental systems adopt for this matter the *lex patriae*, a difference which has led, among other things, to 'double *renvoi*'. But the *lex patriae* test would not be a practical principle for English courts—simple though it is to apply—because the single British nationality embraces a variety of separate legal systems: even United Kingdom citizenship covers more than one system, e.g., English and Scots law.

A wholly satisfactory definition of domicile is probably impossible to formulate; but for practical purposes one may say that his domicile is the place where a person is deemed to have his habitation fixed—he has no present intention of moving from it, and, when away, he intends to return to it. As Lord Cranworth put it, the domicile is a person's 'permanent home'.

In that sense, a person whose place of origin is England could obviously have a domicile in any part of the world. Such a proposition, however, won only a gradual acceptance. Problems of domicile first became prominent in questions arising between England and Scotland and with the development of the empire, so that the courts tended to develop their principles of domicile in relation to habitation *within British territory.* The possibility of a domicile outside British soil for a British subject was recognized by 1823;[1] but there was an underlying tendency in such cases to require a virtual *de facto* naturalization of the person in the state concerned. A clear manifestation of this attitude may be seen in *Moorhouse v. Lord,*[2] where it was suggested that a British subject, to acquire a domicile in a politically foreign state, must *quasi exuere patriam* (as it were, shed his nationality).

In *Udny v. Udny,*[3] however, Lord Westbury stated the principles of the modern English law of domicile. He distinguished the concepts of nationality and domicile; the former gives one a political status, while domicile is the test of one's status in the

[1] *Thornton v. Curling* (1824) 8 Sim. 310
[2] (1863) 10 H.L.C. 272
[3] (1869) L.R. 1 Sc. & D. 441

field of personal law. This destroyed the nationality 'fence' within which the law of domicile had hitherto developed. His Lordship then went on to demonstrate that everyone has a 'domicile of origin' acquired at birth—from one's father, if one be legitimate; from one's mother, if illegitimate—which can never be shed. It can, though, be superseded in active operation by a 'domicile of choice', acquired by residence in another state with the intention of permanent residence there. But, if the domicile of choice be abandoned, the domicile of origin resumes in full vigour unless and until another domicile of choice be obtained. This last is not the only, nor necessarily the best, way of ensuring that everyone has at all times a domicile, the law of which may be referred to in questions involving one's personal status. Indeed, the Private International Law Committee has recently advocated the adoption of the American rule that an existing domicile shall continue until another be acquired, in place of the present rule of revival of the domicile of origin.[1] But unless and until the Committee's recommendation is given statutory effect, in English law the domicile of origin revives upon the abandonment of a domicile of choice.

This durability of the domicile of origin, and the fact that it is attributed to one by law, tend to make it difficult to supersede in some circumstances. For instance, in *Ramsay v. Liverpool Royal Infirmary*,[2] Bowie, a Glaswegian by birth, went to live in Liverpool in 1891 and remained there until his death in 1927. He frequently said that he never intended to leave Liverpool and had stated that he would not return to Glasgow. But, during his life, he described himself as 'a Glasgow man'—an expression that also appeared in his will—and took a weekly Glasgow newspaper. The House of Lords held that he died domiciled in Scotland, never having acquired a domicile of choice elsewhere.

Domicile of origin being thus ever-present, at least in the background, attention may be turned to the question of domicile of choice. For the acquisition of a domicile of choice, there are necessary two factors:

(a) residence in the state in which a domicile is alleged to be acquired

[1] Cmd. 9068, published February 1954; H.M.S.O.
[2] [1930] A.C. 588

(b) the intention of permanent residence there.

But, though both are necessary, intention is the more vital requirement. For *Ramsay's* case shows that long residence of itself is not enough; contrariwise, 'it may be conceded that if the intention of permanently residing in a place exists, a residence in pursuance of that intention will establish a domicile'.[1]

Such intention may, moreover, exist even though the residence is known to be terminable and likely to be terminated. For instance, in *Cruh v. Cruh*,[2] an alien who had come to England before the war, joined the army but was discharged for criminal offences, imprisoned and recommended for deportation—a recommendation which the Home Secretary intended to implement as soon as practicable. The alien sought a divorce and the court took jurisdiction, holding him domiciled in England.

Again, the intention need not exist at the time of taking up residence in the chosen country. The court is concerned to know only the place of domicile at the time relevant for the question before it. For instance, in a succession case, the court wants to know where the deceased was domiciled at his death: when he became domiciled there is of no importance. Similarly, when a petition for divorce is presented, the court's concern is to know whether the petitioner is now domiciled in England. Consequently, 'a domicile of choice can be inferred notwithstanding the fact that the individual to whom it is ascribed is not conscious of having taken any deliberate decision at any given or particular moment'.[3]

Moreover, the domicile being of choice, *ex hypothesi* the intention must be freely formed. Accordingly, the mere fact that, e.g., a political refugee has fled from his homeland for another state does not necessitate his acquisition of a new domicile, any more than would the departure of a chronic invalid from England for the warmth of the Riviera. But conversely, such reason for the change does not prevent the establishment of a new domicile. It all depends upon the freedom of choice possessed by the individual making the change of residence. Upon all the evidence available, the court has to decide whether the person whose

[1] *Bell v. Kennedy* (1868) L.R. 1 Sc. & D. 307, 319 per Lord Cranworth.
[2] (1945) 62 T.L.R. 16
[3] *Gulbenkian v. Gulbenkian* (1937) 54 T.L.R. 241

domicile is in question did, at the relevant time, have the necessary intention, freely formed, of establishing himself in the new state.

Again, since it is a domicile of choice, the person must be legally capable of making a choice: which bars infants, lunatics, and married women from the acquisition of such a domicile. Until the age of twenty-one or, in the case of a daughter, until marriage before that age, the infant is dependent upon its parents for its domicile, having whatever domicile they have at any given time. Further, on reaching twenty-one, it retains the last domicile so received from the appropriate parent (father, in the case of a legitimate child; mother, in the case of a bastard), until a domicile of choice is acquired in the usual way. Of course, this may soon be effected. Suppose that the son of a domiciled Englishman emigrated at seventeen to Australia; he remains domiciled in England unless and until his father acquires a domicile elsewhere: but, as soon as he reaches twenty-one, there is no reason why he should not be held immediately to be domiciled in the Australian state in which he has settled.

On marriage, a woman receives her husband's domicile and thereafter is domiciled wherever he is, so long as the marriage subsists. In *Lord Advocate v. Jaffrey*,[1] for instance, a woman who had spent all her life in Scotland nevertheless died domiciled in Queensland, where her husband, who had deserted her, had settled and, indeed, bigamously remarried. Similarly, a widow retains her husband's last domicile until she acquires one of choice for herself on the usual conditions: *Re Wallach*.[2] But here again, suppose a woman living separate from her husband (who has a Spanish domicile) in France; though herself domiciled in Spain at his death, she might immediately thereafter be held domiciled in France.

The dominant position of the father and husband in this matter of domicile has become the subject of some criticism in this age of ever greater equality of the sexes. After the father's death, for instance, an infant's domicile does not automatically change upon a change of domicile by its widowed mother. If, say, the mother remarried to a person domiciled in France, the child would not necessarily thereby become French-domiciled.

[1] [1921] 1 A.C. 146
[2] [1950] 1 All E.R. 199

If the child lives as a member of its mother's household, it will receive whatever domicile she may acquire, so long as such change will not operate to the child's detriment;[1] otherwise, it would retain the last domicile received from its deceased father. No similar qualification limits the father's power to change his child's domicile. Again, on divorce, the ex-wife, like the widow, will retain her former husband's domicile until she acquires one of choice; and infant children of the marriage, probably, continue to be dependent upon their father for their domicile, although custody of them be granted to their mother. There would seem to be much force in the suggestion that the mother should, upon the termination of the marriage (whether by death or divorce), have the same power of changing the domicile of infant children as had the father, if she in fact has their custody.

A lunatic retains the last domicile that he had before becoming insane, no matter what changes of residence he may make. That, however, assumes that he was at some time capable of rational choice. If he became insane during infancy, it would seem that he remains throughout life dependent upon his father and thus, no matter how long he survives him, will retain the last domicile received from his father: *Sharpe v. Crispin.*[2]

Domicile is a concept also invoked in connection with the artificial persons known in law, i.e., those associations of individuals which, being constituted in the appropriate manner, are regarded as themselves legal entities distinct from their members. In England, such bodies may be created only by royal charter or under statutory authority, e.g., under the Companies Act 1948. Other countries have their own provisions and, by reason of this, English private international law refers to the law of the place where the corporation is alleged to have been created to ascertain whether it is to be regarded as a distinct legal entity.

That law is also the *lex domicilii* of the corporation. Hence, to know, for example, whether a French corporation is able to make this or that contract, reference would be made to French law. Similarly, the sale of shares in an English company would

[1] cf. *Potinger v. Wightman* (1817) 3 Mer. 67 and *Re Beaumont* [1893] 3 Ch. 490

[2] (1869) L.R. 1 P. & M. 611

be regulated by the constitution of the company framed under the Companies Act 1948. Juristic persons are treated so far as possible as natural persons; but, in this matter of domicile, there is a difference—a corporation cannot change its domicile; that is to say, it is always governed by the law of its domicile of origin (which, incidentally, is also its *lex patriae*).

But, especially with trading corporations, other matters than status questions arise. Corporations make profits which states tax; and it may be that, though domiciled in state A, a corporation does most of its business in state B. Recognition of this fact and also of the fact that the income tax law of the United Kingdom places a greater burden upon the profits of those resident in this country than on those making profits here but resident abroad, has led English courts to determine the residence of corporations for fiscal purposes by reference to the place where the control of the business of the corporation lies. The fact that it is, e.g., a German corporation by constitution will not prevent its being resident in England if the board of directors, etc., are centred in London. Such a test is not unreasonable when, by reason of the comparative laxity of the law of incorporation in some states, bodies may be created in those states for the purpose of doing business elsewhere. An unfortunate possibility, though, for the corporation, is that there may be a considerable amount of business control centred in a number of states, in which case it may find itself paying tax more than once in respect of the same profits, etc. This possibility was contemplated with equanimity by the Court of Appeal in *Union Corporation v. I.R.C.*[1]

[1] [1952] 1 All E.R. 646; and by the House of Lords, [1953] A.C. 482

CHAPTER TWO

FAMILY LAW

TURNING from general principles to the particular topics of private international law, it is convenient to consider first the position of the family—the relationship of husband and wife, of parent and child, and the quasi-parental protection which the law provides for those who, through infancy or lunacy, are incapable of looking after themselves.

A. HUSBAND AND WIFE

(*i*) *The Concept of Marriage*

Some form of union of men and women is known in all legal systems. The present concern, however, is with that relationship which, in English law, is recognized as creating two parties man and wife and in respect of which English courts will give matrimonial relief—divorce, maintenance orders, etc. This relationship, in the classic words of Wilde J.O. in *Hyde v. Hyde*,[1] is 'the voluntary union for life of one man and one woman, to the exclusion of all others'.

Though designated a 'Christian marriage', this merely means that English matrimonial law may be invoked only in respect of the type of marriage known in western civilization, i.e., monogamous union. In *Brinkley v. A.G.*,[2] the court recognized a marriage celebrated with Japanese ceremonies in Japan, on being satisfied that, in that country, persons may lawfully have only one spouse at a time. And, in determining whether a marriage is monogamous in character, the court is solely concerned with the nature of the union at its inception. For instance, the ease with which a divorce may be secured by either party is of no account, so long as neither may legally take another consort while the marriage subsists. In *Mehta v. Mehta*,[3] indeed, the marriage ceremony of an Indian Hindu was held monogamous because the sect

[1] (1866) L.R. 1 P. & D. 130, 133
[2] (1890) 15 P.D. 76
[3] [1945] 2 All E.R. 690

of Hinduism, to which he then adhered, practised monogamy, although he could, apparently, by mere act of will, have reverted to orthodox Hinduism and polygamy. Marriage then to the English lawyer signifies a union of one man and one woman which, at its inception, excludes the possibility of either taking another spouse so long as that marriage shall continue.

But there are in the world many people whose personal law allows them more than one spouse. In India and Pakistan, the Hindu and Moslem are governed by their religious law; and Islam and orthodox Hinduism permit a plurality of consorts. Does the English view mean that, e.g., a marriage entered into in India by a Hindu there domiciled would not be recognized in English courts?

To that question, a complete answer cannot as yet be given. Certainly, there are not lacking in the older cases suggestions that such a union would be wholly devoid of effect in English eyes: in more recent years, perhaps reluctance to stigmatize half the world as living in concubinage has produced some changes. In 1939, the House of Lords held that the son of an Indian Hindu peer who had in fact married only once was entitled to his father's seat in the House; a question which depended on his legitimate birth and thus on the validity of his father's marriage.[1] Later, in *Baindail v. Baindail*[2] the Court of Appeal held that his previous polygamous marriage in India disqualified a Hindu from later marrying at a register office in England. Both decisions, however, were cautious. The Lords emphasized that they were deciding only a question of the membership of their House. The Court of Appeal expressly refused to give an opinion whether the Hindu marriage might be regarded as a marriage for other purposes, e.g., to ground a charge of bigamy against the respondent in respect of his attempt at a subsequent English marriage.

The view here taken is that polygamous marriages should be denied recognition only where the English concept of marriage is of necessity involved in the question before the court. Thus, to refuse to grant matrimonial relief to the parties to a polygamous marriage is perfectly defensible; the English law of divorce, etc., concerns monogamous unions. Similarly, provision in the

[1] *Sinha Peerage Claim* 1939 H.L. Jour. Vol. 171, 350
[2] [1946] P. 122

English law of succession for the 'surviving spouse' must contemplate a widower or widow of a monogamous union. On the other hand, an English court might well regard children born of a polygamous marriage, which is valid in the domicile of the parties to it, as born in wedlock. In short, where the question of marriage arises incidentally to some other issue, the court should not feel constrained to adhere rigidly to the English concept of marriage.

Whether a marriage is polygamous in character or not is determined by the *lex loci celebrationis*, the law of the place where the marriage is celebrated. Thus in England only monogamous marriages may be lawfully contracted, even though the parties or one of them be persons whose personal law allows polygamy: *Chetti v. Chetti*.[1] If, by the *lex loci celebrationis*, it is possible to marry either polygamously or monogamously, it will depend upon the law governing the form of ceremony used: Christians marrying in India, for example, would clearly enter into a monogamous marriage.

(*ii*) *Requirements of a Valid Marriage*

Marriage is a matter of both contract and status: that is to say, the parties take each other as husband and wife by contracting each to live with the other; but, once the contract is made, the rights, duties, etc., of the married state are attributed to them automatically by operation of law. To create the status, however, the first requirement is a valid contract of marriage. And just as in any other contract, the parties must have capacity to contract one with the other and also they must make this contract in the appropriate form.

Questions of capacity to marry are determined by reference to the *lex domicilii* immediately before marriage of the party concerned. Thus, if A at eighteen marries B in, say, Spain but, by the law of A's domicile, the marriage of persons under twenty-one is forbidden, an English court would hold the marriage void on the ground that A had no capacity to marry B. The leading authority is *Sottomayor v. De Barros* (1),[2] where the Court of Appeal, on the assumed facts that the parties, who married in

[1] [1909] P. 67
[2] (1877) 3 P.D. 1

England, were domiciled in Portugal, by whose law they could not marry without a papal dispensation, held the marriage would be void.

It has been urged in recent years that capacity should be determined by the law of the place where the parties, at marriage, intend to establish their matrimonial domicile, which in the absence of any clear intention should be presumed to be the domicile of the husband at the time of marriage. To this view, it may be objected that capacity is, *ex hypothesi*, something which must exist before the actual contracting of a valid marriage. Until marriage, each party has still a separate domicile and it would be anomalous to accord governing power to a law which is only potentially the personal law of both. This could be a matter of great importance in an age when, at any rate in some states, marriage requirements particularly reflect the public policy of the state concerned, e.g., in the bans on interracial marriages of some of the American states or the former anti-Semitic legislation of Germany. It might seem that a view which could perhaps obviate such restrictions is wholly commendable: it would be no good, however, if the state or states with which the parties in fact have the closest ties refused to recognize the apparent marriage. It might, indeed, produce even greater hardship, e.g., for the children of the union. Finally, the bulk of authority is in favour of the rule as stated at the beginning of the last paragraph.

To the rule so stated, however, there is an unfortunate exception. If the marriage is celebrated in England where one of the parties is domiciled, then an incapacity imposed upon the other by the law of his/her domicile does not affect the marriage, if it would be effective under English law. For this English law is indebted to *Sottomayor v. De Barros* (2).[1] After the Court of Appeal decision, it was found that the husband was in fact domiciled in England and the case came on again to see whether this made any difference. It was held that it did and that the marriage was after all valid. First cousins may lawfully marry in English law, so the wife's incapacity in Portuguese law was irrelevant. In principle, this qualification is regrettable for its effect is that, in the last resort, the ability of a person to marry in

[1] (1879) 5 P.D. 94

England someone domiciled in England is governed by English law, an inroad on the basic principle which English law does not allow to foreign jurisdictions. In *Pugh v. Pugh*,[1] for instance, it was held that the English requirement that parties to a marriage must be at least sixteen invalidated a marriage in Austria between an English soldier and a Hungarian girl of fifteen, who was domiciled in Austria and eligible by both Austrian and Hungarian law to marry. The Englishman's statutory incapacity[2] to marry a person under sixteen followed him abroad.

Even though the parties may have capacity as above determined, they must both genuinely contract their union and do so in the proper form. Thus, if there be a lack of true consent, the parties will not become husband and wife. In *Hussein v. Hussein*,[3] an English girl of eighteen was terrified by his threats into going through a marriage ceremony with an Egyptian much older than herself: her fears, depriving her of true volition, rendered the ceremony ineffective. Similarly a mistake as to the nature of the ceremony or induced by the fraud of the other party would enable the mistaken person to deny the efficacy of the ceremony on the ground that he or she did not freely consent to that union.

The basic rule is that the *lex loci celebrationis* governs the manner in which a marriage is to be celebrated, as was illustrated in *Kenward v. Kenward*,[4] where the Court of Appeal held void a marriage alleged to have been contracted in Archangel, because certain consents, declarations, etc., required by Soviet law, had been omitted. This principle is recognized even though the place of celebration admits a form unknown in English law. Thus a marriage in the Argentine, at which the bride, then domiciled and resident in England, was represented by a proxy, was held formally valid by the Court of Appeal.[5] Indeed, the House of Lords has recently recognized a marriage which, though formally defective when celebrated, had subsequently been validated by the *lex loci celebrationis*. A and B went through a religious ceremony of marriage in Austria in 1945 when, under then Austrian law, such ceremony was insufficient to create a

[1] [1951] P. 482
[2] Age of Marriage Act 1929
[3] [1938] P. 159
[4] [1951] P. 124
[5] *Apt v. Apt* [1948] P. 83

lawful marriage. In 1949, by reason of Austrian legislation, the marriage became validated in Austria: their Lordships held that it thereby became a valid marriage in English eyes also.[1]

Certain modifications of the rule, mainly for the benefit of British subjects, exist. In the first place, it may happen that there is no local form or, at least, none appropriate to the parties, in the place of marriage. For instance, two Christians domiciled in England may wish to marry in a place where the only local form is polygamous or some barbaric rite: or two Catholics in a wholly Protestant country. In such cases, English courts recognize a so-called 'common law marriage'. For this, the only requirement would seem to be that the parties should agree to live with each other in monogamous union. *Regina v. Millis*[2] was thought to establish that the presence of an episcopally ordained clergyman was necessary: in that case, an Anglican had purported to marry before a Presbyterian minister in Ireland where the local form was Roman Catholic, and the marriage was held a nullity. That decision, however, proceeded upon a mistaken view of the canon law in England: it can scarcely be supposed that Henry VIII accepted a post-Reformation provision of the Council of Trent, on which the decision was based. In any event, the effect of *Millis* was confined to England and Ireland by *Wolfenden v. Wolfenden*,[3] where a marriage between two Canadians in remote China before a Church of Scotland missionary was held valid. And, as marriage requirements in England and Ireland are now regulated by statute, *Millis* is in fact defunct.

As a priest of the Established Church is no longer necessary for the celebration of a valid common law marriage, it would seem a fair inference that no clergyman at all is necessary in his pastoral role (though his presence would naturally be useful as providing a witness that the parties did in fact make the agreement which alone seems essential). This indeed appears from a recent somewhat extraordinary example of a 'Christian marriage'. The Privy Council in *Penhas v. Eng*[4] held valid as a common law marriage a union contracted in Singapore between a Jew and a

[1] *Starkowski v. A.G.* [1954] A.C. 155
[2] (1844) 10 Cl. and Fin. 534
[3] [1946] P. 61
[4] [1953] A.C. 304

non-Christian Chinese, both British subjects, in the presence of some friends; the ceremony was composite, the husband observing the ritual of his own religion and the wife those of her belief.

Other situations are provided for by the Foreign Marriages Acts 1892 and 1947. Replacing the old wartime concept of 'marriage within the British lines', it is enacted that a marriage between persons at least one of whom is a member of H.M. Forces or otherwise employed in foreign territories (as designated by Order in Council) may be celebrated by a chaplain or other person authorized by the Commander-in-Chief and shall be valid as though solemnized in England. These provisions cover not only service personnel but also, e.g., members of control commissions, N.A.A.F.I., etc., allowing them to marry in English form abroad.

The same statutes further provide generally for marriage in English form by persons one of whom at least is a British subject, by appointing Ambassadors, consuls and such British representatives as Marriage Officers, at whose official residences the ceremony may be performed. The details are beyond the scope of this book. But it may be noted that, when both parties are British subjects, the fact that the marriage would not be recognized by the *lex loci celebrationis* is irrelevant. It remains to mention that the Acts are concerned only with the formalities of marriage —each party must still have capacity according to the law of his or her domicile: moreover, they only concern the use of English forms in a foreign country.

There is little authority concerning marriages at sea. Marriages on a British warship on a foreign station are covered by the Foreign Marriages Acts. For the rest it is thought that, if a marriage is performed on a ship on the high seas in a manner which would constitute a common law marriage or is recognized by the law of the place where the ship is registered, it would be formally valid.

(*iii*) *Effects of Marriage*

Marriage being the pre-eminent personal relationship, it might seem that all questions relating to the marital status should be governed, so far as English courts are concerned, by the law of the matrimonial domicile. Some qualification of this principle, however, is inevitable. For example, commercial convenience surely requires that the incapacity, imposed in some states on married women, to make contracts should not invalidate a contract governed by a legal system which does not have this provision. And, even where only the spouses themselves are affected, public policy restricts the scope of application of the personal law of the parties. That a man should not be allowed, say, to beat his wife in England even though his domiciliary law permits such chastisement, is understandable; but, as marriage laws themselves conspicuously reflect the policy of the enacting state, there is a strong tendency—in England no less than elsewhere—to apply the *lex fori* to many questions of the husband and wife relationship, as will be seen in the discussion of matrimonial causes. But, subject to this proviso, it may be said that the general rule is that incidents of matrimony are governed by the personal law of the spouses. And the immediate effects of their marriage—e.g., whether it revokes prenuptial wills,[1] whether the wife takes her husband's name, etc.—are determined by the law of the place where, at marriage, they intended to establish their matrimonial domicile.[2]

One important instance of the operation of the general principle concerns the effect of their marriage upon the rights of the spouses over their movable property in the very common case where they have made no contractual arrangement on the subject. So far as immovables are concerned, the law of the place where the land is situated would, of course, be decisive.

In English law, since the Married Women's Property Act 1882, husband and wife retain separate ownership of their respective property, in the absence of some other arrangement by settlement. But, in many modern foreign systems, where there is no contractual provision, the law itself confers rights on the parties in each other's property—e.g., that anything acquired by either spouse after marriage (other than by gift or inheritance) shall become the joint property of both.

In English private international law, the immediate effect of their marriage upon the property rights of the spouses is deter-

[1] cf. *Re Martin* [1900] P. 211 and Chapter Five post.

[2] See *De Reneville v. De Reneville* [1948] P. 100. Normally this will be the place where the husband is already domiciled at marriage.

mined by the law of the matrimonial domicile for movables and, as said, by the *lex situs* in respect of immovables. Authority for both propositions is to be found in *Welch v. Tennent.*[1] Two domiciled Scots married; the woman owned movables in Scotland and land in England which she gave to her husband, but, matrimonial differences having arisen, she sought to revoke her gift. By Scots law, gifts between husband and wife were always revocable but that rule did not exist in English law. In the House of Lords, Lord Herschell said,[2] 'the rights of the spouses as regards movable property must . . . be regulated by the law of Scotland, but it is equally clear their rights in relation to heritable estate (the land) are governed by the law of the place where it is situate'. Accordingly, the gift of land was held not to be revoked. Suppose therefore that a woman domiciled in Germany, owning freehold land in England, married a man domiciled in England who owned shares in French companies and had a bank account in Italy; they would retain separately after marriage their own property, for English law would govern the land as the *lex situs* and the movables as the law of the matrimonial domicile.

If, during their married life, the couple change their domicile, their rights in movables become subject to the law of the new domicile, i.e., the law of the domicile for the time being is the governing law. Thus, in *Lashley v. Hog,*[3] a Scotsman domiciled in England married a domiciled Englishwoman. As a result of their later becoming domiciled in Scotland, the House of Lords held that the wife became entitled to a half-share in the husband's movable property, in accordance with Scots law.

It is thought, however, that the law of a new domicile cannot operate to divest either spouse of rights of property already acquired under the law of a previous domicile. It would be grossly unjust if, by changing their domicile, a husband could deprive his wife of an interest in his property which she possessed under the law of an existing domicile. The true principle is this: In the absence of a marriage settlement, the law of the matrimonial domicile for the time being governs the respective rights of the spouses in movable property; subsequent acquisitions are

[1] [1891] A.C. 639
[2] at p. 646
[3] (1804) 4 Paton 581

governed by the law of the domicile operative at the time of their acquisition. Thus, suppose that a woman domiciled in New York married a man domiciled in Holland, who owned shares in a German company and had money on deposit at a Rotterdam bank. By Dutch law, all movables belonging to either spouse at marriage and future acquisitions become joint property. Later the couple became domiciled in England where the husband established a business. The wife would, from marriage, become entitled to a half-share in what the man then had and what he acquired thereafter while they remained domiciled in Holland, but would have no claim in the profits of the English business.

If, on the other hand, the parties make a settlement to regulate their post-nuptial property rights, normal contractual principles, in general, prevail.[1] Capacity so to dispose of immovables is governed by the *lex situs* of the land in question; the ability to bring movables into a marriage settlement is governed, like capacity actually to marry, by the immediate pre-marriage domiciliary law of the party concerned.[2] This represents a divergence from the suggested usual rule that capacity to contract is governed by the proper law of the contract,[3] but the divergence is justified as the settlement is an incident of the status relationship, marriage. Suppose then that Miss A, domiciled in Germany, is marrying B, a domiciled Spaniard, in Paris and wishes to bring into a settlement which they draw up in Paris some Italian land and money in a London bank; her capacity to do so will be determined by Italian and German law respectively.

For the formal validity of a marriage settlement, the rules are the same as for an ordinary commercial contract. Consequently, so far as it affects immovable property, it must satisfy the formal requirements of the *lex situs* of the property. A settlement of movables, however, will be formally valid if it complies with the formal requirements of either the law of the place where the settlement is made or the proper law of the contract. The former alternative is a manifestation of the old principle, *locus regit actum*. *Van Grutten v. Digby*[4] illustrates the

[1] For contract, see Chapter Three post.
[2] cf. *Viditz v. O'Hagan* [1900] 2. Ch. 87
[3] Post, p. 82
[4] (1862) 31 Beav. 561

sufficiency of compliance with the proper law: a domiciled Englishwoman, before her marriage to a domiciled Frenchman, executed in France a settlement of English movables, which satisfied the formal provisions of English but not of French law. It was held that, as English law was the proper law of the contract, the fact that the settlement was in English form was sufficient.

The validity of the actual content of a settlement of immovable property would, of course, be governed by the *lex situs*: in the case of movables, however, the proper law of the contract determines the matter. The parties may, in accordance with principle, choose the law to regulate their matrimonial property and, if they do not, then the court has to determine which system of law they must be presumed to have selected. In that case, the presumption is in favour of the domiciliary law of the husband;[1] but it is not conclusive and may be rebutted in favour of some other system. In *Re Fitzgerald*,[2] for instance, a settlement made in Scotland in Scots form between a domiciled Scotswoman and her prospective husband, a domiciled Englishman, disposed of the income of the property in Scots legal terminology; Scots law was taken to be the proper law of the settlement.

If the spouses have made a valid contract in accordance with these principles, then, certainly, so far as concerns movables affected, the settlement will govern their property relations throughout the duration of the marriage, regardless of any change of domicile which they may make. This appears from *De Nicols v. Curlier*.[3] There the House of Lords, treating the provisions of French law for the regulation of matrimonial property as an implied contract between the parties, held that these provisions still governed the rights of a French married couple after they had become domiciled in England. This decision is, in fact, of considerable importance; for, if other foreign matrimonial régimes on coming before the English courts were treated similarly as implied contracts, it is clear that the general principle, that, subject to contract, the law of the domicile for the time being governs marital property relations, would be enormously qualified.

The *lex situs* determines the effect, if any, of a change of

[1] e.g. *Duke of Marlborough v. A.G.* [1945] Ch. 78
[2] [1904] 1 Ch. 573
[3] [1900] A.C. 21; ante p. 27

domicile upon the rights of the spouses in settled immovables. But, in the case of English land, the contractual rights of the parties are unaffected by changes of domicile: *De Nicols v. Curlier* (2).[1] Thus suppose that a couple marry in Spain with a marriage settlement governed by French law, whereby they agree that any property acquired by either is to become the joint property of both; they later become domiciled in England where the husband buys an estate in Hertfordshire. He will, in English law, be treated as holding the estate on behalf of himself and his wife in equal shares.

(*iv*) *Matrimonial Causes*

Though the Christian marriage is, in conception, a union for life, the possibility of its termination has in fact long been recognized. Questions may also arise concerning the validity of a marriage; or, without dissolving their marriage, the spouses may wish to be released from the normal obligation of cohabitation. For such purposes there exist the proceedings styled matrimonial causes, of which the most important in English law are suits for divorce, decrees of nullity or judicial separation in the Supreme Court[2] and the less august proceedings in the magistrates' courts for maintenance and separation orders.

Only with the passing of the Matrimonial Causes Act 1857 did England acquire an ordinary high court competent to declare the termination of a marriage. Until then, such matters were dealt with in the diocesan ecclesiastical courts: every diocese had its court, administering the canon law of the Church of England, with jurisdiction over everyone residing in the diocese. This ecclesiastical origin of English matrimonial law was of great importance in the development of the private international law of divorce and nullity, though modern statutes have wrought a considerable simplification in a topic long confused.

A divorce decree unequivocally terminates a valid marriage, while the grant of a decree of nullity suggests that the parties never were married, though the concept of the voidable marriage

[1] [1900] 2 Ch. 410

[2] The petition for restitution of conjugal rights and the old action for jactitation of marriage (seeking a decree of perpetual silence to prevent the other party from falsely boasting that he or she is married to the petitioner) have now virtually lost all significance.

in modern law somewhat obliterates the distinction. However, both affect the existence of the marital status and will therefore be considered before the lesser remedies.

(*a*) *Divorce*

Before 1857, no English court was competent actually to terminate a validly contracted marriage, the Church having retained the Catholic principle of the indissolubility of marriage. Only Parliament, by a private Act, could release the influential from the bonds of matrimony. Thus, in private international law, English courts were concerned only with the circumstances in which a foreign divorce would be recognized in England. Since divorce dissolves a status and since the English principle is that the domiciliary law governs questions of status, it was early decided that only a divorce granted by the domicile of the parties would be recognized in England. And, when the Divorce Court was established in 1857, the domiciliary principle became also the basis of English jurisdiction, though there were early suggestions —based upon the example of the ecclesiastical courts—that the residence of the parties in England should suffice to permit the Court to grant a decree.[1] The general rule of the exclusive competence of the domicile, however, was finally established by *Le Mesurier v. Le Mesurier*,[2] where the Privy Council, holding the courts of Ceylon incompetent to dissolve the marriage of a person, resident in that island but domiciled in England, said, 'the domicile for the time being of the married pair affords the only true test of jurisdiction to dissolve their marriage'. Clearly, with such a test of jurisdiction, it would be the *lex domicilii* of the parties which governed the divorce.

That a wife has the same domicile as her husband, however, could produce obvious hardship, e.g., in the case of a deserted wife, which minimizes the attractiveness of this broad and basically sound rule. Considerable modification of the exclusive jurisdiction of the domicile has, in consequence, appeared in England—as, indeed, in other common law countries—in modern times, affecting both English divorce jurisdiction and the recognition in England of foreign divorces.

[1] cf. *Niboyet v. Niboyet* (1878) 4 P.D. 1
[2] [1895] A.C. 517

The basic rule is still that English courts have divorce jurisdiction if the parties to the suit are domiciled in England. For the wife petitioner, however, statutory concessions have been made. By the Matrimonial Causes Act 1937, s.13, it was provided that a woman might petition an English court for divorce, although her husband might be domiciled outside the United Kingdom, if he deserted her or was deported from the United Kingdom and, immediately before the desertion or deportation, was domiciled in England. This provision would relieve many cases of undoubted hardship; and virtually all possibility of hardship has now been removed by the Matrimonial Causes Act 1950. Section 18, besides re-enacting the earlier provisions, empowers a woman generally, if she has been ordinarily resident in England for three years immediately preceding the divorce suit, to petition in an English court. For the female petitioner, in short, three years' ordinary residence in England is as good a ground of English jurisdiction as an English domicile: indeed, one might almost describe it as a statutory domicile. The meaning of 'ordinary residence' is not without difficulty as a matter of abstract definition; in practice, an affirmative answer to the question, 'Has her home in fact been in England for the three years?', would suffice, even though she may, say, have gone on a three months' Riviera holiday or spent a year on business in New York.[1]

Whenever an English court is entitled to entertain a petition whether at common law on the ground of domicile or under these statutory extensions,[2] the law applicable is English law. Thus a person may seek a divorce in England only on a ground authorized by English law, i.e., adultery, cruelty, desertion without cause for three years, insanity and (in the case of a wife's petition) certain sexual offences by the husband. Further, if competent to deal with the actual divorce petition, an English court may settle also the other problems which frequently arise, e.g., award damages against the co-respondent when the petition is based on the wife's adultery, make an order for the custody of the children, order the husband to pay the former wife maintenance, etc.

[1] cf. *Stransky v. Stransky* [1954] P. 428.

[2] Other extensions were made by the temporary Matrimonial Causes (War Marriages) Act 1944, which, however, becomes *functus officio* on 31 May 1955.

The first inroad upon the principle that only a divorce granted by the domicile would be recognized in England was a relatively minor one. In *Armitage v. A.G.*,[1] a woman domiciled in New York obtained a divorce in South Dakota. It appeared that, though the divorce would not have been granted in New York, it would have been recognized in that State; for that reason, it was held that it must be regarded as valid in England also. The decision has been criticized but would seem to reveal common sense and accord with principle. If the law of the domicile—which, in English jurisprudence, governs matters of status—regards a person as unmarried, then so should England.

Then, by legislation, Parliament has provided for the exercise by certain British territories of divorce jurisdiction in respect of persons domiciled in England.[2] The lands principally concerned at present are Northern Ireland, Kenya, Singapore, Malaya and Hong Kong, but their number may be increased by the extension of the statutes by Order in Council. The courts of these territories may grant a divorce on any ground authorized by English law to British subjects domiciled in England, if the petitioner is resident in the territory concerned at the time of presenting the petition and the parties last resided together there. It need hardly be said that divorces granted under these Acts will be recognized in England.

In view of the wide jurisdiction conferred on the English courts by S.18 of the 1950 Act, however, far the most important development has been the acceptance of the principle that English courts will recognize a divorce granted by a foreign court, which took jurisdiction in circumstances similar to those in which an English court might grant a decree, even though the parties were not domiciled in the foreign state concerned. In *Travers v. Holley*[3] a man domiciled in New South Wales left his wife in Sydney and had probably lost his domicile there when she petitioned the New South Wales court for a divorce on the ground of his desertion. It appeared that New South Wales has a statutory provision similar to that which allows deserted wives to petition in England.

[1] [1906] P. 135

[2] Indian and Colonial (Divorce Jurisdiction) Acts 1926–1940; Colonial and Other Territories Divorce Jurisdiction Act 1950.

[3] [1953] P. 246. Cf. *Dunne v. Saban* [1954] 3 All E.R. 586

The Court of Appeal held that the Australian divorce must be recognized here: it would, said the Court, be contrary to principle not to recognize a decree given on the basis of a jurisdiction which England herself claimed. In an age when many common law states have recognized the difficulties which the common domicile of husband and wife may place in the path of a female petitioner, this readiness to accord recognition to a decree essentially similar to one which might have been granted in England is wholly laudable, though it clearly cuts down the exclusive competence of the domicile.

Hitherto, the discussion has assumed the granting of a divorce by a court. There are, however, places where divorce is not a matter of judical decree: e.g., in Quebec, dissolution of marriage may be effected only by legislation, while in Demark divorces are granted by the King and, under Jewish and Mohammedan religious law, the husband may divorce his wife by his own repudiation carried out in the proper manner. Great importance attaches to this because a suggestion was made in the *Hammersmith Marriage Case*[1] that only divorces granted by a court could be recognized in England. There the court held ineffective an attempt by an Indian Mohammedan to divorce the wife he had married at an English register office by *talak-nama*, a declaration of divorce allowed by Mohammedan law. The true ground of that decision, however, was that, being celebrated in England, the marriage was monogamous and an English court could not recognize its termination by a procedure designed for polygamous relationships. That is a perfectly sound principle which enables us to ignore the previous suggestion. It would be intolerable if, e.g., England were to refuse recognition to a divorce obtained in Denmark from the executive by a domiciled Dane.

The true principle, it is thought, is this: English courts will recognize as valid any dissolution of marriage effected in the manner authorized by the domiciliary law of the spouses, provided that it is appropriate to the character of the marriage. Thus, in *Har-Shefi v. Har-Shefi*,[2] the court held valid the dissolution of a monogamous Jewish marriage by a *gett* (letter of divorce author-

[1] *Rex v. Hammersmith Superintendent Registrar of Marriages, ex parte Mir-Anwaruddin* [1917] 1 K.B. 634

[2] [1953] P. 161 and [1953] 3 W.L.R. 200

ized by Jewish religious law) delivered in London, because it would be effective in Israel where the spouses were domiciled. In the same way, it is thought, a Mohammedan divorce would, in a proper situation, be accepted here. Suppose that a domiciled Indian of Mohammedan faith, having a wife already in India, met in England an Englishwoman whom he wished to marry: if he delivered a *talak-nama* to his Indian wife, he should then be regarded as divorced and fully capable to remarry in England.

(*b*) *Nullity of Marriage*

English law takes a distinction between a *void* marriage—one which in truth was never a marriage at all, and a *voidable* marriage —one which does exist but may be terminated on the petition of one of the parties to it, through some fault present at its inception.[1]

A marriage is void when there was some defect in the contract of marriage which the parties purported to conclude, for only upon a valid celebration can the marriage status arise. Hence, a marriage is wholly void if the parties are lacking in capacity to marry each other,[2] or if either does not freely enter into the union,[3] or the proper formalities have not been observed.[4]

A marriage is voidable when, although the contract cannot be impugned, some factor exists which prevents the full and proper relations of husband and wife between them. The original ground of voidability derived from the ecclesiastical control of matrimonial proceedings. As the Church regarded consummation as essential to the marital status, impotence was a ground on which the annulment of the union might be sought. This was taken over by the Divorce Court in 1857 and further grounds of voidability were added by the 1937 Act. A marriage is now voidable in England on any of the following grounds:

(i) impotence of either spouse

[1] Save in the case of wilful refusal to consummate, introduced as a ground of nullity and not as (more properly) one of divorce by the Matrimonial Causes Act 1937.

[2] e.g., *Pugh v. Pugh* [1951] P. 482

[3] e.g., *Hussein v. Hussein* [1938] P. 159; *Mehta v. Mehta* [1945] 2 All E.R. 690

[4] e.g., *Kenward v. Kenward* [1951] P. 124

(ii) wilful refusal of the respondent to consummate the marriage

(iii) that either spouse at marriage was of unsound mind,[1] a mental defective or subject to recurrent epilepsy

(iv) that the respondent at marriage had communicable venereal disease

(v) that the respondent at marriage was pregnant by someone other than the petitioner.

These grounds may, in a sense, be claimed to affect consent—X will, presumably, intend to marry someone who will perform all wifely functions towards him or, if aware of all the facts, would demur to fathering another's child or risking infection. But, in truth, so long as each party intends to be linked with the other who is in fact standing at the altar with him or her, the existence of a sufficient consent cannot be denied. These defects really affect the status of marriage, not the contract, and so, more properly, fall to the category of dissolution. Only the fact that they must exist at the inception of the marriage gives colour to their classification as bases of nullity.

There is a clear difference between flaws in a contract and flaws in a status. But the Church courts used the same form of decree for annulling both void and voidable marriages, declaring the marriage always to have been void. This form—necessary because the courts had no power to terminate marriages—led to both types of ground being regarded as of equal effect and nature. Again, the Church courts based their competence on the residence of the parties within the diocese and were little troubled by choice of law problems, being governed by the canon law. Meanwhile, in the lay courts, the principle was emerging that the domiciliary law governed a person's status, while the *lex loci contractus* received great prominence in matters of contract. When matrimonial jurisdiction was transferred to a lay court in 1857, the combination of the influences of the old ecclesiastical practice and of the existing secular principles made for some confusion in the private international law of both jurisdiction and choice of law in nullity suits. Thus instances might be found of English courts taking jurisdiction because the marriage was celebrated

[1] In the case of complete insanity, of course, the marriage would be void, for the insane person would be incapable of genuine consent.

in England[1] or the parties were resident here,[2] and applying English law to decide the issue even though the parties were domiciled elsewhere.[3] To trace the development of tolerably clear principles from this welter of conflicting tendencies would require a book of greater scope; the present concern will be to consider the main current principles.

On principle, it might seem reasonable that a person claiming that his or her marriage is void should be able to obtain a decision on the matter from the court of any state where he or she happens to be. English courts, however, do not take so liberal a view of their jurisdiction and will entertain such a petition only in certain circumstances.

A decision that a marriage is void is clearly a declaration of the status of the persons concerned, for bachelordom and spinsterhood are status no less than marriage. In consequence, an English court would certainly hold itself competent to adjudicate upon a petition in a case where the parties are domiciled in England. Indeed, it is sufficient that only the petitioner is domiciled in England. Of course, in the case where the petitioner is the female party to the contested marriage, the male being domiciled in some other state than England, this raises the difficulty that, by reason of the common domicile of husband and wife, the petitioner should surely be deemed to be domiciled with the respondent until her claim is established. Logic, however, here yields place to convenience, for otherwise the petitioner might be obliged to travel halfway round the world to confirm that she is a single woman. So, in the case of a petitioner who is in fact living in England in such circumstances that, if the marriage be void, she would be domiciled here, the court will take jurisdiction. *White v. White*[4] affords an illustration. An Englishwoman, while visiting Australia, met and 'married' a man domiciled in either Victoria or Malta. Two days after the ceremony, she returned alone to England where she had since remained and now petitioned for a nullity decree on the ground that the man was already married at the time of the Australian ceremony. If so, of

[1] cf. *Simonin v. Mallac* (1860) 29 L.J.P.M. & A. 97
[2] cf. *Hutter v. Hutter* [1944] P. 95
[3] *Hutter v. Hutter* supra.
[4] [1937] P. 111

course, the ceremony had been meaningless for lack of capacity: Bucknill J. took jurisdiction and granted a decree.

Again, since grounds of voidness allege flaws in the contract of marriage, English courts exercise nullity jurisdiction on such grounds, if the marriage impugned was celebrated in England—an application of the principle, *locus regit actum.*

Where the court is competent to take jurisdiction, the choice of law depends on the nature of the contractual defect alleged, in accordance with the principles discussed in section (ii) ante. Thus questions of capacity and consent are governed by the domiciliary law, immediately before marriage, of the party concerned,[1] while issues as to formalities are referred to the law of the place of the ceremony.[2]

As the grounds on which a marriage is voidable in English law are all matters affecting the status of marriage, it would be consistent with principle if English courts took jurisdiction on such grounds only where the parties are domiciled in England. Recent decisions suggest that at common law this is in fact so, subject to one modification. The leading authority is *De Reneville v. De Reneville.*[3] A domiciled Englishwoman married a domiciled Frenchman in Paris; after cohabiting with him in French territory, she left him and returned to England where she now sought a nullity decree on the grounds of his impotence and wilful refusal to consummate the marriage. The Court of Appeal refused her a decree, holding that an English court could not take jurisdiction. In English law, these grounds made the marriage only voidable and, since no evidence of a different view in French law was produced, it must be presumed that they had the same effect in that system. The woman thus became the wife of the respondent on marriage and was now domiciled in France.

The modification referred to is essentially the principle underlying *White v. White.* The Court of Appeal said, in the *De Reneville* case, that, if the petitioner could have shown that, by French law as the law of the matrimonial domicile, the grounds on which she based her petition would make the marriage void, then she

[1] cf. *Sottomayor v. De Barros* (1), *Pugh v. Pugh, Hussein v. Hussein* ante, and *Way v. Way* [1949] 2 All E.R. 959

[2] *Kenward v. Kenward* ante.

[3] [1948] P. 100. See also *Casey v. Casey* [1949] P. 420

could have claimed to be domiciled in England, and the court would have been competent on that basis.

Foreign legal systems, however, do not necessarily take the same distinction between void and voidable marriages as that of English law. Even with the concession in *De Reneville's* case, therefore, a female petitioner might, at common law, find herself subjected to difficulties similar to those of the woman petitioning for divorce, because of the common domicile of spouses. Section 18 of the 1950 Act, however, applies also to a wife's petition for a nullity decree,[1] so that the woman who has been ordinarily resident in England for three years need not concern herself with the problem of her domicile in seeking a nullity decree in an English court. The male petitioner, though, must always satisfy the court that he is domiciled in England, if he would obtain the annulment of a voidable marriage here.[2] Whether the jurisdiction of the court be based upon the domicile of the parties in England or on the statutory residence of the female petitioner, the law governing the substance of the petition—e.g., deciding what constitutes wilful refusal, etc.—is English law.

The concessions made to the female petitioner by legislation, for nullity no less than for divorce, while doubtless commendable from a municipal English standpoint, may be of dubious merit internationally. It does not follow that, because an English court grants a woman a decree on the ground, say, of her husband's impotence, the decree will be recognized by the courts of other states, including that of the husband's domicile. There is, in short, great danger of their aggravating the problem of the 'limping marriage'; that is, the marriage whose existence is asserted by the courts of one state and denied by another.

So far as the converse problem of English recognition of foreign nullity decrees is concerned, it is thought that the danger of the limping marriage is reduced to the narrowest limits possible, consistently with principle. In the first place, a nullity decree

[1] Section 18 is applicable in respect of both void and voidable marriages but its principal importance is in relation to voidable ones; for it is in respect of them that, at common law, the domiciliary courts are exclusively competent.

[2] Cases suggesting that, at common law, the residence of the parties in England should be sufficient to ground English jurisdiction, on the analogy of the old ecclesiastical jurisdiction, cannot stand with the principle upon which the decision in *De Reneville v. De Reneville* is based.

granted by the domiciliary courts will be acknowledged in England, whatever the ground of the petition. Thus, in *Salvesen v. Administrator of Austrian Property*,[1] the House of Lords conceded the validity of a Wiesbaden decree, granted to a Scotswoman who had resided there for some twenty-six years with her 'Austrian husband', on the ground that the parties had failed to comply with the requirements of French law at the time of their marriage in Paris. For the rest, it may be said, on the authority of *Travers v. Holley*,[2] that a decree granted in circumstances in which an English court would have been competent to grant one will be recognized here. Substantial similarity of the basis of jurisdiction and of the ground of petition will ensure English respect for a foreign decree. Hence our courts would regard as valid a decree granted in, say, some American state to a woman, who had been three years resident there, on the ground of the impotence of her French-domiciled husband. In the absence of the ideally desirable, but unlikely, international legislation on divorce and nullity jurisdiction, recognition of decisions of the domiciliary courts and of such other decrees as go no further than England's own infringements of the exclusive competence of the domicile, would appear the most satisfactory possible course.

(*c*) *Judicial Separation and Other Matrimonial Relief*

As a decree of judicial separation only terminates the normal duty of cohabitation, without affecting the status of marriage itself, there is no call for the exclusive jurisdiction of the domicile. Indeed, whether married persons should live together is essentially a question for the place where they are resident and, accordingly, English courts assume competence to make such a decree if the spouses are resident here.

Apart from this jurisdiction of the superior courts, the

[1] [1927] A.C. 641 : cf. *Galene v. Galene* [1939] P. 237—recognition of French decree annulling marriage of French-domiciled couple, even though the marriage was celebrated here and valid in English law.

[2] [1953] P. 246, ante p. 59. In the earlier *Mitford v. Mitford* [1923] P. 130, Duke P. recognized the validity of a German decree granted in circumstances similar to those of *Mehta v. Mehta*, ante p. 45—lack of consent of petitioner, ground of petition; German jurisdiction as place of celebration of the marriage.

magistrates' courts in England are empowered to make orders for separation and/or maintenance between spouses who are resident in England, even though their domicile is in some other state.[1] For the exercise of this jurisdiction, it is generally necessary that the husband, no less than the applicant wife, be resident in England, on the normal principles of personal jurisdiction.[2] Hence no order could be made against a man who, leaving his wife penniless here, has gone to live in, say, France. It would, however, no longer be possible for him to escape his liabilities merely by crossing the border, for the Maintenance Orders Act 1950[3] provides that such orders may be made in England, on the application of a wife resident in England, against a man resident in Scotland or Northern Ireland, if the last place of common residence was England.

The performance of marital obligations is so much a matter for the place where the parties are resident that public policy must inevitably influence to a considerable degree the question of recognizing decrees and orders of this type made in another jurisdiction. In general, however, subject to that consideration, it is thought that an order, made in a state where the parties were at the time resident, should be recognized in England. In the case of maintenance orders, there is the further difficulty that such orders are usually subject to variation if the parties' circumstances alter and so would not be 'final' judgments in the sense necessary to ensure their acceptance and enforcement in England.[4] Within the British family of nations, this last obstacle has been overcome by statutory provision for the enforcement in one part of the Commonwealth of an order for maintenance made in the courts of another.[5] Ideally, it would be desirable that similar provision be made for foreign orders generally. Such a step by our Parliament could not, however, fairly be expected without reciprocal arrangements by other states—of which, at present, there is no sign.

[1] Summary Jurisdiction (Separation and Maintenance) Acts 1895 to 1949.
[2] Chapter One, ante.
[3] This Act does not affect separation orders.
[4] cf. Chapter Six post.
[5] Maintenance Orders (Facilities for Enforcement) Act 1920: the provisions of the Act now apply to most parts of the Commonwealth and Empire with the exception of India and Pakistan, and the Province of Quebec.

B. Parent and Child

In English municipal law until 1927, the only parent-child relationship recognized was the legitimate link—that created by the birth of the child in lawful wedlock to the alleged parents. A bastard, technically, has no parents and, before the Legitimacy Act 1926, could not be legitimated; bastardy was an indelible stigma. Likewise, before the Adoption Act 1926, no artificial parent relationship could be created which produced any legal effect. As other states have not always shared the English views on these matters, it is clear that private international law problems can arise in this very important field of human relationships.

The question whether a child has been born the legitimate or the illegitimate child of X is essentially a simple one. But, unfortunately, it has usually been raised, in English courts, in actions concerning the disposition of the property of a deceased person, the common case being a claim by A that he is entitled to the property as being the 'heir', 'child', etc., of B deceased. Now, in such a case, the real problem is not the status of any person as such, but the disposition of B's property—who is entitled under the will or intestacy? That depends upon the law governing the succession, i.e., the law of the domicile of the deceased in the case of movable property, the *lex situs* for immovables.[1] Thus, the true question in our example is not really, 'Is A the legitimate child of B?'; but, 'Is A the person entitled to take as a "child", etc., under the law governing B's succession?'. It may be that that legal system recognizes as children only persons with particular qualifications, e.g., that they were born of a marriage celebrated in church, etc.[2] In short, there is no necessary connection between the fact of legitimate birth and the right to succeed to property. As seen in the discussion of the exclusion of foreign law,[3] though a status given by the appropriate law has universal recognition, the incidents of that status depend upon the law under which it is sought to exercise them. That distinction has not, however, always been recognized and courts

[1] See Chapter Five post.

[2] It may be noted that, in English law itself, since the Matrimonial Causes Act 1950 s. 9, legitimate birth is not necessarily based on birth in lawful wedlock in that issue of a voidable marriage are held to be born legitimate, even though the marriage be annulled.

[3] Chapter One ante.

have declared persons not to be legitimate when the real issue was whether those persons were entitled to succession rights under the *lex successionis*;[1] conversely, it has been held that, because he was born legitimate, a claimant was so entitled.[2]

By reason of this merger of issues, it is difficult to find direct authority for any definite principle for determining the status of an individual. But it is clear that, the problem being one of status, the law of a domicile is appropriate to determine the question. The problem then arises, Which domicile? For one's domicile of origin itself depends on one's status at birth. The better view, for which there is judicial support[3] and which is consistent with the general dominance of the father as head of a family, is that the domiciliary law of his alleged father at the time of the child's birth determines whether the child is born legitimate.

The person who does not satisfy this test is born a bastard but that stigma may be removed by the process of legitimation. English law resisted so humane a concept until 1927, when the provisions of the Legitimacy Act 1926 came into force. But in countries which, broadly speaking, based their legal systems on that of Rome, legitimation had long been known in various forms—through the marriage of the parents after the birth of their child (*per subsequens matrimonium*); by the putative father's acknowledgment that the child is his, etc. By reason of its almost universal existence outside the common law, English courts, though they knew no legitimation themselves, were constrained to evolve a rule for determining when they would recognize the validity of a legitimation alleged to have been effected in some other state; for the problem often arose, frequently in claims on an English succession. The rule adopted by English courts may be stated as follows:

A person is recognized in England as having been legitimated if legitimation in the manner asserted was permissible by the domiciliary law of his father both at the time of his birth and at the time of the alleged legitimation.[4]

Thus, in the event of a person claiming that he had been

[1] cf. *Shaw v. Gould* (1868) L.R. 3 H.L. 55
[2] *Re Bischoffsheim* [1948] 1 Ch. 79
[3] cf. *Re Grove* (1889) 40 Ch.D. 216, 224; *Re Luck's Settlement Trusts* [1940] Ch. 864, 883
[4] *Re Goodman's Trusts* (1881) 17 Ch.D. 226

legitimated by the marriage of his parents in, say, France, English courts would accept the claim if his father was domiciled, both at the claimant's birth and at the time of the French marriage, in a state where such legitimation was part of the law.

Satisfaction of this double test was made unnecessary for legitimation by subsequent marriage, by the Legitimacy Act 1926 which introduced legitimation into English law. The Act provides that, where the parents of an illegitimate child[1] marry each other, the father being at the time domiciled in England or Wales, the child is legitimated from the time of the marriage. It is further enacted that, if the father of an illegitimate child, being domiciled *outside* England and Wales, marries the mother, the child shall be regarded as legitimated in England, provided that legitimation *per subsequens matrimonium* is recognized by the father's domiciliary law at the time of marriage.[2]

This simplified test, referring to the domicile at marriage only, applies only in the case of legitimation by marriage, the one form of legitimation known in English law itself. A person asserting that he has been legitimated in any other manner must satisfy the common law rule if his claim is to be upheld in an English court. Thus, in *Re Luck's Settlement Trusts*,[3] the Court of Appeal declined to recognize that the claimant had been legitimated by the acknowledgment of paternity made by his father in California, where he was domiciled, in accordance with the law of that State. At the claimant's birth, the father was domiciled in England, which knew no such legitimation and so the first part of the common law rule was not satisfied. In a way, it is perhaps unfortunate that the common law and statutory principles should exist side by side in this way; the desirability of a single rule for all legitimation is obvious. At the same time, the common law rule has a certain advantage over the statutory rule in that persons legitimated at common law are relieved of the stain of bastardy as from birth while the statutory legitimation operates only from the marriage of the parents. This may be of importance, e.g., in claims to succeed to property under a will which comes

[1] Other than children born in adultery.

[2] S. 8. Children born in adultery are not excluded under this section if they would be legitimated by the father's domiciliary law: *Collins v. A.G.* (1931) 47 T.L.R. 484

[3] [1940] Ch. 864

into operation before the legitimation took place. Consequently, even in the case of legitimation by marriage under a foreign legal system, if the common law rule has in fact been satisfied, then the person concerned is considered to be legitimated thereunder and not under the provisions of the statute.[1]

A person born legitimate, of course, takes the domicile and nationality of his father from birth. A child who has been legitimated will acquire his father's domicile as from legitimation, and, in the case of the legitimated child of a citizen of the United Kingdom and Colonies,[2] his nationality also. The effect of legitimation upon nationality in other countries must, naturally, depend upon the law of the country concerned.

The mutual rights and duties of father and child, whether born legitimate or legitimated, should, perhaps, on principle be determined by their domiciliary law. In an English court, however, the interests of the child are always the paramount consideration, to which any rights of the parent are subordinated.[3] Thus, for instance, though normally the father has the right to custody of his child, an English court would award the care of the child to its mother or some other person, if satisfied that such course was better for the child.[4] Similarly, property of the child in England may be dealt with by the father only in so far as English law permits his administration. In consequence, it can scarcely be said, in this case, that the domiciliary law as such is operative at all. In justification of this attitude, it may be stressed that the protection of the young is so much a matter of public law no less than of private rights that, in the case of conflict, the law of the *forum* must inevitably prevail over the system which normally governs private relations.

The rights of succession existing between parent and child are a matter, as already said, for the law governing the succession. So far as English law is concerned, it is thought that, where such a claim depends on the legitimate birth of some person, then it

[1] cf. *Re Hurll* [1952] 2 All E.R. 322

[2] British Nationality Act 1948, s. 23

[3] Guardianship of Infants Act 1925, s. 1, giving statutory effect to the common law as enunciated in, e.g., *Johnstone v. Beattie* (1843) 10 Cl. & Fin. 42, 114

[4] See, e.g., *Re B's Settlement* [1940] Ch. 54 and cf. *McKee v. McKee* [1951] A.C. 352

must be shown that that person was born in lawful wedlock.[1] A person legitimated under the Legitimacy Act 1926 is granted full rights of succession, as though born in lawful wedlock, under dispositions of property which come into operation after his legitimation,[2] with the now unimportant exception that he cannot claim as an 'heir'.[3] Subject to the same qualification, a person legitimated at common law, however, is treated for this purpose as though never affected by the stigma of bastardy.[4]

As already stated, the illegitimate child has, in English law, technically no parents; in general, though, his mother has the same position as has the father in the case of legitimate issue. Thus it is from his mother that he takes his domicile of origin; it is his mother who normally is entitled to his custody and is responsible for maintaining him.

Principle would suggest that the rights and liabilities, if any, of the natural father are a matter for his domiciliary law. In the important matter of jurisdiction to make orders on the father to contribute to the support of his bastard child, however, the concern of English courts is with the domicile of the mother and the residence of both parents. If the mother was domiciled in England when the child was born—even though it was born outside England—and both father and mother are resident in England, then the magistrates' courts are competent to make an affiliation order on the application of the mother.[5] Thus a domiciled Englishwoman could get an order here against the German-

[1] *Shaw v. Gould* ante: *Re Bischoffsheim* ante, which suggests a different principle is probably wrongly decided and is, anyhow, of inferior authority.

[2] Section 3.

[3] Under the 1925 property legislation, a common set of rules for the devolution of all property on intestacy was instituted. In consequence, heirship is of importance only in the following cases:

(*a*) For the descent of titles of honour;
(*b*) where a direct disposition is made in an instrument to the 'heir' of a person;
(*c*) for the devolution of real property on the intestate death of a person who became a lunatic before 1 January, 1926.

[4] *Re Goodman's Trusts* ante; *Re Grove* ante; *Re Andros* (1883) 24 Ch.D. 637; *Birtwhistle v. Vardhill* (1835) 2 Cl. & Fin. 571; *Re Grey's Trusts* [1892] 3 Ch. 88

[5] Bastardy Laws Amendment Act 1872, s. 3: cf *R. v. Humphreys* [1914] 3 K.B. 1237

domiciled father of the child born to her in Paris, if both he and she are resident in England. As with wife maintenance orders, if the man be resident outside England, the courts here have generally no jurisdiction. But, as between England, Scotland and Northern Ireland, statutory provisions now authorize the making of orders in one country against a man residing in another.[1]

The possible recognition of such orders made in a foreign country is a problem of great importance and one which, at present, is in a most unsatisfactory state. In the first place, English courts in this case do hold that the liability of the father is governed by his domiciliary law.[2] Hence, if by his *lex domicilii* the father were under no duty to support his bastard child, then an order made against him in another state would not be recognized here. Again, such orders normally being variable, even an order made in the father's domicile would not satisfy the requirement of 'finality' which is a prerequisite of recognition, in this country, of foreign money judgments. Further, public policy might prevent the enforcement of a foreign order, as imposing, e.g., too great a liability.[3] The whole question is one which urgently requires consideration but a satisfactory solution would depend upon a degree of international agreement which cannot be anticipated in the near future.

The relationships hitherto considered are natural relationships of parent and child, whether or not their creation has the approval of the law. In 1926, English law for the first time admitted the creation of the status of parent and child between those who were not so related by blood. The Adoption of Children Act 1926 was confined in its operation to children who were British subjects and resident in England and adopters domiciled and resident in England. The scope of adoption has, however, now been extended by the Adoption of Children Act 1950 which authorizes the making of an adoption order in respect of a child who is resident in England; the desirability of providing a proper home life for a child who is in fact residing in England has led to the ouster of the requirement of British nationality or even of an

[1] Maintenance Orders Act 1950
[2] *Coldingham Parish Council v. Smith* [1918] 2 K.B. 90
[3] cf. *Re Macartney* [1921] 1 Ch. 522

English domicile. The adopter, however, must still be domiciled and resident in England.[1]

The effect of adoption in English law is to sever all links between the adopted child and his former family and to make him a member of his adopter's family, as if he had been born into that family. For the purposes of the law of succession, he is in essentially the same position, in relation to his adopter, as a person legitimated under the common law rule.

Forms of adoption are known in other systems of law but vary, both in form and in their consequences, from state to state. English courts have never yet been called upon directly to recognize a foreign adoption. It is, however, generally agreed that they would not recognize such an adoption unless it were valid by both the domiciliary law of the adopter and that of the adopted child, at the time of the adoption. Thus, for instance, whether a domiciled German had in fact adopted an Italian child in Bonn would depend on whether the adoption was possible by both German and Italian law.

The effects of recognition must depend upon the nature of the issue before the court. Principle would suggest that the respective rights of the adopter and adopted child, between themselves, would after a valid adoption be governed by the domiciliary law of the adopter, who would then be as a father to the child. So far as successionary rights are concerned, the law governing the succession will determine their extent; that is, the domiciliary law of the deceased in the case of movable property, the *lex situs* for immovables, would decide whether an adopted child may take as a 'child', etc., of his adopter.[2]

C. Guardianship and Lunacy

From family relations properly so-called, it is but a step to those cases where a substitute for parental care and control is recognized and allowed by law in recognition of the fact that the persons affected are, through lack of years or of mental capacity, unfit to face life without some supervision.

In both cases, the public nature of the responsibility for

[1] He must also satisfy certain requirements as to age and/or kinship to the child; s. 1 (1).

[2] *Re Wilson* [1954] 1 All E.R. 997

the care of such persons being manifest, English courts have a sweeping jurisdiction. Thus, a guardian may be appointed in England for an infant who is a British subject, wherever he may be, and also for any infant domiciled or resident in England, whatever his nationality. The guardian is appointed to the person of the child, the question whether the child has any property being irrelevant. In *Re D*,[1] for instance, a guardian was appointed for a penniless Jewish child of German extraction and domicile who had come to England as a refugee. The person appointed has certain rights and duties in respect of the child—he is responsible for its education, entitled to its custody, and, if it has any property, will administer it as a trustee for the infant's benefit.

Since England claims so wide a jurisdiction, it might happen that there is a child of foreign domicile or nationality who is resident in England, for whom a guardian has already been appointed in his domicile or national state, but in respect of whom guardianship proceedings are taken in England. It is therefore relevant to inquire what weight will be given by English courts to the fact of the foreign appointment.

In itself, the foreign guardianship carries no weight in an English court. The Guardianship of Infants Act 1925 provides broadly that 'in any proceeding before any court . . . the court . . . shall regard the welfare of the infant as the first and paramount consideration'. Hence, whether the question be one of property or of the personal custody, education, etc., of the child, the English court may do whatever it pleases if the course it adopts is considered to be the best thing for the child.[2]

Opposition to a foreign guardian will scarcely be a regular occurrence and, in its absence, it would not be necessary (though it might be desirable) for the foreign guardian to secure confirmation of his position in an English court. It seems clear that, without resort to an English court, he might exercise in this country such rights in respect of the child as could an English guardian—e.g., arrange its education, exercise control over its movements—and administer any movable property in England which is due to the ward, claiming payment of debts owed to the child and suchlike proceedings.

[1] [1943] Ch. 305
[2] See *Re B's Settlement* [1940] Ch. 54; *McKee v. McKee* [1951] A.C. 352

In the case of lunatics also, English courts have wide powers in the matter of their custody and supervision. A committee (a guardian or curator) may be appointed here for any lunatic who either is personally present in England or has property here. Hence, if a person domiciled in one of the United States should become insane while on holiday in England, the court might make provision for him.[1]

Again, as with infant wards, it may be that a foreign curator for the lunatic has already been appointed at his domicile. That would not deprive the English court of its jurisdiction and, if it chose, it might appoint another to act as curator in this country.[2]

If, however, the domiciliary curator is not objected to, or faced with a rival here appointed by the English court, he may, on proof of his appointment, claim control of movable property belonging or due to the lunatic in England, e.g., demand payment of debts due to the lunatic.[3] Without authorization from the English court, however, he could not administer immovable property in England belonging to the lunatic;[4] and his personal powers of control over the lunatic would be limited to those accorded by English law.

[1] *Re Burbidge* [1902] 1 Ch. 426
[2] *Re Houston* (1826) 1 Russ. 312
[3] *Pélégrin v. Coutts* [1915] 1 Ch. 696: certain types of property are regulated by statutory provision, e.g., stock in English companies under the Lunacy Act 1890 s. 134
[4] *Grimwood v. Bartels* (1877) 46 L.J. Ch. 788

CHAPTER THREE

OBLIGATIONS

FOR present purposes, we may say that an obligation is a legal relation between two specific persons, whereby one or each of them is under a duty to comport himself in a particular manner towards the other, for breach of which duty he will be liable to make compensation in damages. The law of contract concerns such duties arising out of agreement: if A and B agree that A shall deliver goods for which B will pay £5, then B may sue A if he does not supply the goods and A may sue B if he does not pay the price. Again, one must not cause physical harm to another, make false statements about him, damage his goods, etc.; for breach of such duties, the law of civil injuries—torts, as the law terms them—allows the aggrieved person to claim damages from the wrongdoer. Quasi-contract is a term denoting circumstances in which, without breach of any contractual or tortious duty, one person has derived a benefit at another's expense which it would be unjust for him to retain: for instance, B owes money to A and by mistake pays it to C—B could recover the money from C in quasi-contract. The private international law rules relating to each of these branches of the law will be separately considered, as also those governing a particular and important type of contract, the negotiable instrument.

A. CONTRACT

It has been said above that the law of contract concerns obligations arising out of agreement. But not all agreements constitute contracts—the parties must be capable of binding themselves to legal duties and must make their agreement in the proper form (if any special form be required); finally, of course, the object of the alleged contract must be valid and legal. The problems of capacity, formalities, and essential validity of the contract are thus raised: in all these connections, the doctrine of the Proper Law of a contract is of the greatest importance.

(i) The Proper Law of a Contract

In English private international law, a contract is governed by its proper law; that is, by the law which the parties intend to govern the promises which they have made. This has been the accepted English doctrine since *Robinson v. Bland*[1] in 1760: a recent statement may be found in the words of Lord Atkin in *Rex v. International Trustee*:[2]

'The legal principles which are to guide an English court on the question of the proper law of a contract are now well settled. It is the law which the parties intended to apply. . . .'

This may be called the Subjective theory of the proper law and is the leading English doctrine. If a Frenchman and a German have made a contract in Italy for the delivery of goods from Turkey to Hungary, payment to be made at a bank in Athens, and they have agreed in the contract that the terms of the contract shall be governed by English law, then, in the event of disputes arising, the claims would be determined by English law. Bearing in mind the number of countries that might be involved in a modern commercial contract, when international trading is commonplace, the principle has much to commend it. Also, from the more insular standpoint of English legal theory, it clearly accords with the conception of contract as an agreement between two free agents: they may choose as they please and the court will enforce their agreement.

To accord the parties free choice is not, however, to grant them an arbitrary licence—that could open the way to abuse of independence. For, by the selection of some wholly unrelated system of law, an attempt might be made to evade the provisions of the law of the countries in which the proposed contract is to take effect. Accordingly, some limits on the freedom of choice were indicated in what is now regarded as the leading authority upon the topic. In *Vita Food Products v. Unus Shipping Co.*,[3] a contract was made in Newfoundland for the shipping of herrings from that territory to New York, in a Nova Scotian ship, the relevant documents providing that the contract was to be governed by English law, the herrings to be delivered in good condition,

[1] (1760) 2 Burr. 1077
[2] [1937] A.C. 500
[3] [1939] A.C. 277

and the shipowners to be exempted from liability for negligence. A Newfoundland statute provided that The Hague Rules (a set of international conditions of sea carriage) governed the carriage of goods on ships sailing from Newfoundland ports and that documents relating to such shipments must expressly state that those Rules were applicable. That statute had not been complied with in the present case. The ship having run aground off Nova Scotia through the master's negligence, the purchasers of the fish now sued the shipowners for damage to the herrings. They argued that, because the contract did not comply with the Newfoundland Act, it was bad and therefore the shipowners could not rely upon the clause exempting them from liability for negligence. On appeal from Nova Scotia, the Privy Council dismissed the claim, holding that the choice of English law was perfectly valid and thus that the exemption clause was valid. But, while confirming by the actual decision the principle of free choice of law, Lord Wright said:

'. . . when the English rule that intention is the test applies, and when there is an express statement by the parties of their intention to select the law of the contract, it is difficult to see what qualifications are possible, *provided the intention expressed is bona fide and legal, and provided there is no reason for avoiding the choice on the ground of public policy*'.[1]

The meaning of his Lordship's closing observations is not, perhaps, entirely beyond dispute; the view here taken, however, is that Lord Wright meant simply that the choice must be such that it would not be contrary to English public policy to enforce it and thus, by inference, posited that the choice must be reasonable, having regard to the circumstances of the case. Businessmen are not idiots—if they choose a system of law to govern their dealings, they have a reason for doing so. Now suppose that a Belgian and a Spaniard make a contract for the delivery of goods from Bruges to Madrid, selecting English law to govern their dealings; suppose further that the evidence shows that under both Belgian and Spanish law dealings in that particular commodity are forbidden but that no ban exists under English law. It would scarcely be difficult to divine the motive of their selection of English law and to say that, by giving it effect, an English

[1] [1939] A.C. 277, 290: the italics are the author's.

court would be assisting in acts prejudicial to friendly foreign states. And refusal to assist parties in such circumstances is a well-established application of the doctrine of public policy. Such, it is thought, is the type of situation which would be affected by Lord Wright's qualification.

If, however, some valid reason for the parties' choice can be discerned—or, indeed, one may say, if no unworthy explanation of it be obviously apparent—then their selection will be respected, even though it might appear that the link between the facts of the case and the law chosen is somewhat tenuous. For instance, in the *Unus* case itself, the choice of English law to govern a commercial maritime contract is perfectly reasonable, when one considers the dominant position which English maritime law attained in the world by reason of our long supremacy upon the seas.

Hitherto, the discussion has concerned the case where the parties make an express choice of the system of law which they wish to govern their contract. It frequently happens, however, that an express choice is not made. In such case, the court has to endeavour to discern the implied or presumed intention of the parties. It must set itself to answer the question, 'Looking at all the circumstances of the case, which legal system might the parties, as reasonable men, be expected to have chosen, had they directed their minds to the matter?'

In this quest, the court has various guides on which, if necessary, it may fall back. For instance, it often happens that, in the absence of an express selection, the court may refer to the *lex loci contractus*: if A makes a contract in Ruritania with B, a domiciled Ruritanian, it may not be unreasonable to suppose that they intended their transaction to be governed by Ruritanian law. Again, in contracts relating to ships—their victualling, refitting, etc.—a reference to the law of the flag, i.e., the law of the place where the ship is registered, would be natural. It should, however, be noted that such guides to the parties' intentions are only pointers and not conclusive: as was recently pointed out in *The Assunzione*,[1] they yield inferences not absolute presumptions.

In the last resort, all the circumstances of the particular contract may be relevant in determining the law which the parties

[1] [1954] P. 150

may be presumed to have intended. For example, in *The Adriatic*,[1] a contract was made in Egypt between A, an Egyptian firm, and B, an English company which had a branch in Egypt, for the shipment of B's goods from Egypt by A to England. A hired a Swedish ship and loaded it with B's goods, the relevant documents being drawn up in English. The ship was damaged on the voyage and had to put into Cadiz as a total loss, and B accepted the cargo there. A now, on behalf of the Swedish shipowners, claimed payment for the distance that the cargo had been carried. This claim would be valid under either Swedish or Egyptian law but not in English law. Langton J. rejected the claim, holding that the proper law of the contract of carriage was English. In the absence of express choice by the parties, the learned judge considered the fact that the documents were drawn in English, that delivery was intended to be made to England, that the defendants, B, were English, that English influence was then thought to be predominant in Egypt where the contract was made. These factors led him to decide that English law must be presumed the proper law of the contract.

It may now be mentioned that, though the subjective theory of the proper law—whether expressly or impliedly chosen—is the rule in English courts, there is a school of thought which maintains that a contract should be governed by the law with which it is most substantially connected; this may be termed the Objective theory. In the light of such cases as *The Adriatic*, it may be seen that this theory is most useful in ascertaining the *presumed* intention of the parties, when they have omitted to make an express selection of the governing law. It cannot, however, be set up as the prevailing and generally operative principle of the English private international rules of contract.

(ii) Capacity

The English rule on capacity to make contracts is not settled, but judicial statements on the question fall into two groups:

(a) those favouring reference to the *lex domicilii* of each party

(b) those referring to the *lex loci contractus*.

It may be observed, however, that the statements in group (a) occur in cases concerning the validity of marriages. As marriage

[1] [1931] P. 241

affects the status of the parties to it, it is proper that capacity problems in such a context should be determined by reference to the *lex domicilii* of the party in question.

But, in dealing with the ordinary commercial contract, strict adherence to the principle of domicile might produce commercially harmful results. In English law, for instance, an infant may not be made liable in respect of a contract made by him for goods that he cannot be said to require, 'non-necessaries'. In England, the infant is a person under twenty-one: surely it would be unfair that a domiciled Mexican aged twenty-four should be able to obtain such goods in England, refuse to pay for them and then, when sued, plead infancy on the ground that, under Mexican law, he does not attain majority until twenty-five.

Such a possibility enables us to see why other judges have sought to invoke the *lex loci contractus* to determine contractual capacity. It may well happen, however, that the contract has no connection with the *locus contractus* except that it was made there. Suppose that a Frenchman and a German, while both on holiday at Lucerne, make a contract there for the delivery of goods from Spain to Italy: is it really satisfactory that any question concerning the capacity of either party to make the contract should depend upon Swiss law?

In truth, both the views considered are unsatisfactory. Accordingly, since no rule has yet been firmly established, it is urged that the most satisfactory test of capacity is the proper law of the contract, as the law governing the substance of the contract generally. In fact, in the cases in which the *lex loci contractus* has been mooted for determining capacity, that legal system would certainly have been the proper law. Moreover, there would fit conveniently with the suggested test the rule that the *lex situs* determines the capacity of parties to a contract for the transfer of land or interests in land: *Bank of Africa v. Cohen.*[1] For dispositions of land have as their proper law the *lex situs* of the land. Again, the possible geographical complexities of a contract indicate the desirability of a single test for questions affecting the substantial validity of a contract. For all these reasons, it is submitted that capacity to make a contract should be governed by the proper law of the contract.

[1] [1909] 2 Ch. 129

(iii) Formal Validity

The original principle was a direct application of the maxim *locus regit actum*, viz., formalities of contract are governed by the *lex loci contractus*. Hence, for example, if the law of Utopia requires that contracts for the sale of goods should be in writing, then such a contract between a Frenchman and an Englishman made in Utopia would have to be in written form to rank as an effective agreement, so far as English courts are concerned. But, with the development of the proper law principle, it has become accepted that, even though it may not satisfy the requirements of the *lex loci contractus*, the contract will nevertheless be formally valid if it does comply with the provisions of the proper law. The present position, therefore, is that a contract will be held formally valid if it satisfies the provisions of either the *lex loci contractus* or the proper law. Hence, if an Egyptian and an Italian made a contract in Paris, expressly to be governed by English law, use of the form appropriate under either French or English law will ensure that the contract is recognized, as to form, in an English court.

(iv) Essential Validity

The actual substance of the contract—the nature of the duties assumed by either party, the extent of those obligations, etc.—is, of course, governed by the proper law. It goes without saying that, if the contract be found invalid under that law, then no effect will be given to it in an English court. In *Heriz v. Riera*,[1] A and B, two Spaniards in Spain, agreed that A, who had a contract to supply the Spanish government with tobacco for five years, should give a share of the profits to B. This contract would be illegal under Spanish law, as B was an official of the government. Accordingly, when an action was brought in England to recover B's share from A, the claim was rejected: the contract was void under its proper law, that of Spain. Similarly, in the modern case of *Zivnostenska Bank v. Frankman*,[2] a claim for money due under a contract governed by Czech law was rejected by the House of Lords on the ground that, under Czech law, the defendants could not pay without getting per-

[1] (1840) 11 Sim. 318
[2] [1950] A.C. 57

mission therefor from the Czech National Bank, which permission had been refused.

It has been seen earlier that, by reason of the public policy rule, England will not enforce the performance of an act which might endanger our relations with friendly foreign states. It consequently happens that, although a contract may be valid by its proper law, it may yet not be enforced in England, if its performance would be invalid by the law of the place where that performance is due to take place. In other words, the provisions of the *lex loci solutionis* may affect the validity of acts to be performed under the contract. In the *Ralli Brothers* case,[1] an agreement had been made in London for the carriage of jute from Calcutta to Barcelona, the cost of carriage to be £50 per ton, payable as to half in London and as to the other half in Barcelona by the recipients: the contract was governed by English law. Before the cargo reached Barcelona, the Spanish government had decreed that the maximum carriage rate for jute should be 875 pesetas per ton, much less than the agreed £50. When the ship arrived, the Barcelona recipients tendered only 875 pesetas per ton, the then legal maximum in Spain. The shipowners now sought to recover the balance of the contract rate of £50 per ton. The Court of Appeal rejected the claim. It would have been illegal in Spain to pay more than 875 pesetas and an action could not be maintained here for failure to break the law of the country where payment was due to be made.

Strictly speaking, this does not mean that the *lex loci solutionis* overrides the choice of the parties. The contract, as such, is not illegal, as would be the case if it contravened its proper law. The present result is due simply to the rule that English courts, as a matter of public policy, will not enforce acts illegal where performance is due.

Provided that the contract is valid by its proper law and that its performance would not infringe the rules of the *lex loci solutionis*, possible illegality under some other system of law with which the parties or the contract may be connected is not material. In *Kleinwort's* case,[2] for instance, an Hungarian bank had guaranteed a debt contracted by their Hungarian client to an

[1] *Ralli Bros. v. Compañia Naviera Soto y Aznar* [1920] 2 K.B. 287
[2] *Kleinwort Sons & Co. v. Ungarische Baumwolle* [1939] 2 K.B. 678

English creditor, payable in London. When the date for payment passed, the English creditor sued the bank on its guarantee. The defendants pleaded that Hungarian exchange laws made it illegal for Hungarian nationals to pay money outside Hungary without the consent of the Hungarian National Bank and that they had been unable to obtain such consent and thus could not pay without committing an offence under Hungarian law. The Court of Appeal held this irrelevant: the proper law of the contract was English and England was the place of performance of the obligation; there was nothing illegal about payment of this debt in English law and the claim accordingly succeeded.

Kleinwort's case raised a problem which has become of prime importance in the international money obligations of the modern world, that of currency control legislation. So far as concerns those states which are parties to it, the Bretton Woods Agreement of 1945 makes a provision which has, through legislation, become part of English law.[1] By its terms, 'exchange contracts which involve the currency of any member and which are contrary to the exchange control regulations of any member maintained or imposed consistently with this agreement shall be unenforceable in the territories of any member'. Thus, any contract which offends the exchange laws of any member state would be given no effect in England. Regulations of states which do not subscribe to the agreement will receive effect only in accordance with the normal rules, i.e., if the law of the state concerned is the proper law of the contract or the *lex loci solutionis*.

The general subject of money obligations may be briefly adverted to. The English rule is that, whatever the proper law of the contract, if a debt is expressed to be due in a given currency, then the debtor's obligation is to pay the nominal amount of the debt in whatever is legal tender under the law of the state of that currency at the time that payment becomes due; regardless of variations in the currency since the making of the contract. For instance, in *Re Chesterman's Trusts*,[2] a debt of 30,000 German marks had been contracted before World War I when the mark was of sound value and on the gold standard; the debt fell due

[1] Bretton Woods Act 1945 and S.R. & O. 1946, No. 36
[2] [1923] 2 Ch. 466

after the war when Germany was in the throes of inflation and 30,000—now paper—marks were worth no more than elevenpence: it was held that payment of this paper rubbish was a valid discharge of the debt. Similarly, if the mark had doubled in value by the time that the debt fell due, it would still have been necessary to pay 30,000 marks. This rule—the principle of nominalism, as it is termed—does not infringe the paramountcy of the proper law as the governing law of the contract. On the contrary, indeed, it is a necessary complement to it. The obligation to pay the amount in the currency concerned is created under the proper law; only the law of that currency can say what constitutes the currency at the date for payment. Suppose, for instance, an agreement expressly subject to French law whereby X promises to pay Y on 20 April 20,000 lire; French law determines whether a valid obligation to pay the lire has been created: to ascertain that X is in truth discharging his obligation so created, when he makes a tender on 20 April, recourse must be had to Italian law to ensure that the money offered is in truth 20,000 lire. The nominalism principle thus ensures compliance with the obligation engendered under the proper law.

B. Negotiable Instruments

A negotiable instrument is a particular type of contract in writing for the payment of a sum of money. Originating in international commercial practice, to facilitate the transfer of payments and creation of credit between businessmen of different states, it has a striking characteristic which marks it off from other contractual documents—that the person to whom it is transferred, and who receives it in good faith and for value given by him, obtains—by the fact of transfer—a better right to claim the money promised by the document than is possessed by his transferor. The result is that the instrument is itself usable almost like money. English law determines for itself to what instruments it concedes this effect. The typical negotiable instrument, however, is the bill of exchange, defined in the Bills of Exchange Act 1882 (hereafter called simply 'the Act') as 'an unconditional order in writing, addressed by one person to another, signed by the person giving it, requiring the person to whom it is addressed to pay on demand, or at a fixed or determinable future time, a sum certain of money to, or to the order of, a specified person, or to bearer'.[1] A common, if rather special, form of bill is the cheque.

As a unit of international currency, as it were, the bill of exchange can obviously raise problems of private international law. It may, for example, be drawn by a Frenchman in Paris on Smith in London in favour of Hans, a German. Moreover each transfer or indorsement itself constitutes a contract between the indorser and the new holder in due course, which again may be affected by foreign elements. In our illustration, Hans may indorse the bill in Switzerland to Pietro, an Italian, who later indorses it in Spain to Juan, who finally presents it for payment to Smith in England. The negotiable instrument is thus the focal point of a series of separate contracts, each of which may raise private international law questions.

The problem is to know by what law each stage of such a series of transactions is governed, a task towards which some contribution is made by section 72 of the Act. Since the matter is contractual, the previous classification of the elements under the heads of capacity, formalities and essential validity may be used.

(a) Capacity

The Act makes no specific provision for determining who may be a party to a bill of exchange. It might therefore seem proper to invoke the general rule relating to contractual capacity, which, it was suggested, is the proper law of the contract. There is, however, this difference between the present topic and contract in general—that, in relation to negotiable instruments, the Act appears to discard the proper law principle and tends very decidedly to resort to a fixed criterion, the law of the place where the transaction in question was effected, i.e., the *lex loci contractus*. It is, therefore, thought that capacity to be a party to a bill of exchange—whether in the actual making or in one of the supervening contracts effected by indorsement—depends upon the *lex loci contractus*, the law of the place where that particular transaction is effected.

(b) Formalities

Section 72 (1) of the Act provides as a general principle that

[1] Section 3 (1)

the formal validity of a bill is governed by the law of the *place of issue*, and of indorsements by the law of the place where they are made. Thus a bill issued in France will be regulated as to its form by French law. A word of explanation, though, is necessary as to 'place of issue'. Being a connecting factor no less than, e.g., domicile, the place of issue is defined by English law: and in an English court a bill is held to be issued in the place where it is delivered, not merely made. So, if a bill were drawn in France on an English bank and posted to the payee in Southampton, it would be regarded as delivered and thus issued in England: it would, consequently, have to comply with English formal requirements, e.g., as to the stamp duty payable. The rule relating to indorsements is illustrated by *Koechlin v. Kestenbaum*,[1] where a bill payable in England had been indorsed in France by an agent of the payee without his signing himself '*per pro.*' the payee, as would have been necessary under English law. The indorsement, however, was valid under French law as it stood and thus the Court of Appeal held that payment must be made to the indorsee.

To the general rule, there are, however, certain exceptions. In the first place, English courts would not regard a bill issued outside the United Kingdom as invalid merely because it was not stamped in accordance with the law of the place of issue.[2] If, say, a bill drawn and delivered in Paris in favour of a German and payable in Spain did not bear the stamps required under French law but was satisfactory in other respects, it would be held formally valid in this country.

Again, if a bill issued outside the United Kingdom would in fact satisfy English formal requirements, then, although not complying with the law of the place of issue, it would receive effect in England for the purposes of payment as between any English parties to it. Suppose a bill issued in France on an English bank in favour of a Spaniard who indorsed it to an Englishman. Although it did not satisfy French law in its form, the indorsee would yet be able to demand payment in England, if it conformed to the English provisions governing the form of bills. But the Spaniard, the original payee, would not have been

[1] [1927] 1 K.B. 889
[2] Bills of Exchange Act 1882, s. 72 (1) proviso (a)

able to obtain similar satisfaction. This is a rather unfortunate provision making for, as it were, divisible validity of a bill. As is seen in the example, the acceptor, though not liable to the original payee, could become liable to an indorsee. The problem will recur in connection with essential validity.

(c) *Essential Validity*

The essential validity of a bill and its interpretation, as also of any supervening contract, are governed by the *lex loci contractus*:[1] that is to say, the legal effect of the bill and of each indorsement (if any) is governed by the law of the place in which that transaction is effected.

Such is the general rule, from which will be seen the rigidity introduced by the Act in place of the flexibility of the proper law doctrine. A bill drawn in China on a drawee in France and payable in London is to be governed by Chinese law! In illustration may be cited the great case of *Embiricos v. Anglo-Austrian Bank.*[2] A cheque was drawn in Roumania on a London bank in favour of L. E., who, still in Roumania, indorsed it to G. E., a London firm, and put it in an envelope to send to G. E. The cheque was stolen from the envelope by a clerk of L. E. It was subsequently presented for cashing at the S & S Bank in Vienna, bearing what appeared to be a regular indorsement by G. E. but was in fact a forgery. S & S in good faith cashed the cheque and then indorsed it in turn to the A-A Bank in London and posted it to them. A-A cashed the cheque at the London bank on which it had been drawn and were now sued for conversion of the cheque by L. E., the original payees. The ground of the claim was that a forged indorsement could not give title and thus that the A-A Bank had wrongly used the cheque to obtain money to which L. E. rightfully had title. That would have been so, had the matter of the Viennese transaction been governed by English law. By Austrian law, on the other hand, a holder in good faith of a cheque, for which he had given value, did become entitled to it, even though prior indorsements on it might have been forged. Two of the judges, who dismissed L. E.'s claim, did so on the ground that, under the Act, the validity of the indorsement

[1] Bills of Exchange Act 1882, s. 72 (2)
[2] [1905] 1 K.B. 677

fell to be determined by Austrian law as the law of the state where the transaction took place.[1]

It will be seen that the action in the *Embiricos* case was between two payees, i.e., the original payee and an indorsee. The question whether the parties in an action concerning a bill of exchange are payees, payers, etc., may be very important in litigation for reasons now to be considered.

It must be mentioned, in the first place, that a distinction is taken between an *inland* bill and an *outland* or *foreign* bill. An inland bill is one drawn and payable in the British Islands (e.g., a bill drawn by a Glasgow merchant on a French acceptor to be paid at a London bank); or one drawn in the British Islands on someone there resident (e.g., a bill drawn in Douglas, I.O.M., on a Northern Ireland bank in favour of a Parisian). All other bills are foreign.[2]

Now, as a proviso[3] to the general rule referring validity to the *lex loci contractus*, it is provided that, where an inland bill is indorsed in a foreign country, the indorsement shall, as regards the payer, be interpreted according to the law of the United Kingdom.[4] This enacts the previously existing common law and may be exemplified by the old case of *Lebel v. Tucker*.[5] There a bill had been drawn, accepted and was payable in England: it was indorsed in France in a form which satisfied English law but was not a proper indorsement according to French law. The Court of Queen's Bench, however, held that an acceptor of an English bill agrees to honour an order which would be valid in England and accordingly decided that the acceptor must pay the French indorsee.

The effect of the proviso, it will be seen, is to make the liability of an English payer subject to English law and thus to introduce again the possibility of divided liability noticed in connection with formalities. Assuming the facts of *Lebel v. Tucker* to arise again since the Act, the position would be that the payer would have to pay the indorsee, although—as between the original

[1] The other judges based their decisions on the treatment of the bill as a chattel and thus governed by the *lex situs*, equally Austrian law.
[2] Bills of Exchange Act, s. 4.
[3] s. 72 (2) proviso
[4] The Act applies to bills throughout the United Kingdom.
[5] (1867) L.R. 3 Q.B. 77

payee and the indorsee—there had been no valid indorsement, since French law, the *lex loci contractus*, had not been observed. Conversely, suppose that, in the *Embiricos* case, the bill had been drawn in Scotland instead of Roumania, thus becoming an inland bill, and that the action was by the A-A Bank against the payer instead of being between two payees. In that case, although as between the payees, the forged instrument would be perfectly valid, the payer would not be liable to pay out to the A-A Bank because, by English law, the forgery gave no rights.

It is unfortunate that liabilities may or may not exist in respect of an internationally useful instrument like a bill of exchange in this way. The Englishman is put in the fairly simple position of knowing that duties in respect of a bill which are to be performed in England fall generally to be determined by English law. But it may be doubted whether such insular qualifications provide any real attraction, if one reflects upon the possible international transactions which may arise out of the one instrument. The real solution to the private international law of negotiable instruments is, of course, the adoption, on an international level, of a uniform set of rules. Conventions were in fact made at Geneva in 1930 for the adoption of a uniform law of bills and promissory notes and private international law questions arising thereout and also to co-ordinate rules concerning stamp duties. This country, however, has adopted only the agreement relating to stamp duties, the least important of the group.

C. Civil Injuries

To ascertain whether a person may sue in England for a wrong which he claims to have suffered in another country, English courts have adopted a dual test. In the words of Willes J., in the leading case of *Phillips v. Eyre*:[1]

'As a general rule, in order to found a suit in England, for a wrong alleged to have been committed abroad, two conditions must be fulfilled. First, the wrong must be of such a character that it would have been actionable if committed in England. . . . Secondly, the act must not have been justifiable by the law of the place where it was done.'

The case itself illustrates the operation of the rule. The

[1] (1870) L.R. 6 Q.B. 1, 28

defendant was alleged to have assaulted the plaintiff and subjected him to imprisonment during a rebellion in Jamaica, at a time when the defendant was Governor of that island. Before the action commenced, the Jamaican legislature had passed an Act of Indemnity excusing action taken during the disturbance. The Court of Queen's Bench dismissed the action: though Eyre's conduct constituted the English torts alleged (assault and false imprisonment), it had become validated under the *lex loci delicti*, i.e., Jamaican law, and was thus not unjustifiable in the place where it occurred.

It will be noted that different wording is used in each part of the rule. 'Actionable' in the first part is clear: it obviously means that the conduct must be such as to constitute a tort for the redress of which an action exists in English law; i.e., it must amount to an English trespass, libel or slander, nuisance, etc. This is understandable, in that the action before the English court will have to be framed in one of the accepted English torts.

"Justifiable', the word used in the second half of the rule, is much more imprecise. It does not necessarily suggest that the conduct complained of must be such as to permit the person injured or wronged to claim damages under the *lex loci delicti.* And, in fact, it has been held by the Court of Appeal that the rule is satisfied if the conduct complained of is criminal in the place of commission, although no action in respect of it would lie there. In *Machado v. Fontes*,[1] the plaintiff claimed damages in respect of a libel on him published by the defendant in Brazil. The defence was that, under Brazilian law, no action lay for libel. It appeared, however, that a person publishing a libel would be liable to prosecution on a criminal charge there, and the Court in consequence held the defence insufficient. Being criminal in Brazil, the place of commission, the conduct of the defendant was 'not justifiable' there. This decision has been much criticized on the ground that it permits action in England for tort, when no tort has in fact been committed in the place where the facts arose. Why, ask the critics, should a man be able to get damages in England for an alleged injury which would be unremediable in this manner in the place where it occurred? The bulk of academic opinion favours the proposition that the *lex loci delicti* should

[1] [1897] 2 Q.B. 231

govern tortious liability; the courts, on the other hand, would appear committed to the principle of *Machado v. Fontes* unless and until the House of Lords overrules that decision.

What is really required by the two-fold English tort rule is that the conduct complained of must constitute an English tort and must also be, in some manner, cognizable by the courts of the country in which the conduct occurs. Suppose that A were knocked down by a Ruritanian motorist while on holiday in Ruritania and that, under Ruritanian law, a person injured in a motor accident has no right of action against the driver but may obtain compensation from a central insurance fund. If it be the case that there are no other provisions of Ruritanian law under which the conduct of the Ruritanian motorist could be impugned, then A could not bring an action in England in respect of his injuries; for the motorist's conduct would not be cognizable by the courts of Ruritania. But, if the criminal law of Ruritania made negligent driving an offence and the motorist had been driving negligently when he hit A, then an action in England would be available to A: since he would have to answer for his conduct in the courts of Ruritania, the motorist's conduct could not be said to be justifiable there.

If all the facts on which the English claim is founded occurred in one state, there would obviously be no difficulty in deciding where the wrong was committed. Complications arise, though, if more than one state is involved. Suppose that X in Italy fires a gun and wounds Y who is standing just across the frontier in Switzerland. Are we to say that the wrong is committed in Italy, where the act which caused the injury is done? Or in Switzerland where the injury is suffered which makes the shooting wrongful? For firing a gun would not necessarily be wrongful in itself.

On this question, there is a variety of views: some say that the *locus delicti* is the place where the act is done, while others hold that it is the place where damage is inflicted; others again take the view that the person injured should be able to claim as the *locus delicti* any state in which any of the pertinent facts occurred. It is submitted that the question depends upon the wrong for which the action is brought. It has to be remembered that the claim, as it appears in an English court, is in respect of *an English tort*. Now, the tort of negligence requires an act or failure to act in circumstances in which it could have been foreseen that harm to the plaintiff would result and from which harm has in fact resulted. In such case, it is not surprising that English courts should regard as the *locus delicti* the place where the act or omission occurred. In *George Monro v. American Cyanimid Co.*,[1] the action arose out of the purchase in New York, under a contract governed by New York law, of rat poison to be resold in England. By reason of its defective quality, the purchasers incurred liability in England and now sought to claim against their American sellers for the latters' negligence in providing defective poison. The Court of Appeal indicated their opinion that the tort was committed in New York: that was where the sale took place from which the trouble arose. The essence of libel is the *publication* of the false statement about the plaintiff, i.e., the actual communication of the statement by the defendant to a third person: accordingly, the place of commission is the place where the publication is effected. Thus in *Bata v. Bata*,[2] where a libel had been written in Switzerland but was posted to and read (thus receiving publication) in England, the Court of Appeal was of opinion that the tort was committed in England.

These instances suggest the general principle that the *locus delicti* is the place in which the conduct occurs which constitutes the essence of the tort in respect of which a claim is made. Thus, for instance, in nuisance the essence of the tort is interference with the plaintiff's enjoyment of his land, and therefore the tort is committed—the *locus delicti* will be—in the place where such interference occurs. Hence, if smoke from A's factory on the Scottish side of the border blights B's garden on the English side, the tort, on the view here taken, would be committed in England.

Though, in general, English courts may take jurisdiction in respect of tortious conduct abroad, provided that the English rule is satisfied, there is an important exception. No action may be brought in England in respect of a trespass to foreign land. *British South Africa Company v. Companhia de Moçambique*[3] arose out of a dispute as to the title to a piece of land in South Africa, which was claimed by both British and Portuguese

[1] [1944] 1 K.B. 432
[2] [1948] W.N. 366
[3] [1893] A.C. 602

colonizers. Finally, this action was brought by the Portuguese company claiming redress against the British company for the latter's trespass on the land in question, a claim which would be justified if the territory belonged to the Portuguese. The House of Lords held that the English courts had no jurisdiction to entertain the action. Clearly, title to foreign land was really in issue in the *Moçambique* case and that an English court should refuse to determine ownership of foreign land is understandable. However, the decision stands as authority that no action for trespass at all may be brought in England, if the wrong was committed against foreign land. This is an unfortunate result. It means, for instance, that if A throws a stone through the window of X's house in Calais—without in any way disputing X's ownership of the house—X will be unable to recover against A therefor in England. Yet, if A were to assault him as well as smashing his window, X would be able to sue A in England in respect of the assault.

Torts may, of course, no less be committed on the high seas, e.g., in the case of a collision between two ships outside territorial waters. In such case, liability is governed by the general maritime law, which means, in fact, English law. In short, in a case of this sort, there is no dual test: the municipal law of England governs the matter: *The Leon*.[1]

D. Quasi-Contract

As previously indicated, a quasi-contractual claim lies when one party has received a benefit at the expense of the other, in circumstances in which it would be unjust for him to be allowed to retain it, although its receipt did not give rise to a right of action in either contract or tort. A single comprehensive rule cannot be postulated, for there are three types of situation in which such a claim may arise, each involving a different test.

(*a*) *The claim may arise out of the termination of a genuine contract*

Suppose, for instance, that A and B make a contract, full performance of which becomes impossible through circumstances beyond the control of either: but, before this frustrating event,

[1](1881) 6 P.D. 148

B has paid A some money under the contract or incurred some expense in at least beginning to perform his side of the bargain. He has thus commenced to benefit A without getting anything in return, though—at the same time—A is under no contractual duty to him, for it is not A's fault that the contract has gone off. B wishes to recover from A the amount that he has paid or the expense to which he has been put. By what law should the validity of his claim be determined?

Reason and authority suggest that the proper law of the erstwhile contract should be the governing law. Thus, in the *Fibrosa* case,[1] the facts were that an English company had, in 1939, agreed to supply and deliver in Poland, to the plaintiffs, a Polish company, machinery for their factory. The price was £4,800 of which £1,600 was payable in advance, and the plaintiffs had in fact paid £1,000 on the making of the contract. Before any machinery could be delivered, the Germans had overrun Poland and—England being at war with Germany—obviously the delivery could not thereafter take place. The plaintiffs then sought the return of their £1,000, having received nothing for it. The proper law of the contract had been English law, and the House of Lords, in finding for the plaintiffs on their present claim, applied the principles of English law. Similarly, it is thought, a claim to recover money paid by mistake in discharge of a contract governed by French law would be determined according to the principles of French law.

(*b*) *The claim may arise in connection with land*

In such case, general principle requires that the claim should be governed by the *lex situs*, the law of the place where the land in question is situate. Suppose that the tenant of land in France wishes, at the end of his tenancy, to claim from his landlord for improvements which, he says, he has made in the land during his tenancy: his success will depend on whether such a claim is allowed under French law. Thus, in *Batthyani v. Walford*,[2] the Court of Appeal allowed a claim in respect of Hungarian land, because it was countenanced by Hungarian law: the present

[1] *Fibrosa Spolka Akcyjna v. Fairbairn Lawson Combe Barbour Ltd.* [1943] A.C. 36

[2] (1887) 36 Ch.D. 269

tenant of the land was claiming against his predecessor on the ground that the latter had derived a greater benefit from the land than he was entitled to and had transmitted the land to the plaintiff in a condition inferior to that in which he had received it.

(*c*) *The claim may arise in circumstances unconnected with contract or with land*

In such a case, it is thought that the law of the place where the enrichment took place should govern the claim. Suppose that A, a Frenchman, intending a gift to B, a Dutchman, pays into the London bank account of another Dutchman, C, by error, £200. English law would determine whether A could recover the money on finding his error.

CHAPTER FOUR

LAW OF PROPERTY

FROM obligations, we turn to consider the principles applicable in questions involving proprietary interests—as, for instance, whether such-and-such a contract made in Italy was effective to transfer a plot of land in Germany from A to B: or whether X can claim in London from Y, who resides there, a debt the right to which Z purported to assign to X in Brussels. Strictly speaking, the law of succession forms part of the law of property; but it comprises so large a body of substantive principles of its own as to merit separate treatment hereafter. Thus this chapter will be essentially devoted to discussion of the problems which may arise from transactions *inter vivos* (between living persons) in respect of property rights. However, both *inter vivos* and on succession, the question of first importance, upon which all else depends, is the nature of the property, interests in which are concerned.

A. THE NATURE OF PROPERTY

In a case which concerns questions of ownership or other proprietary interest, the first question which the court must answer is whether the subject-matter of the interest is immovable or movable. In a literal sense, of course, the question whether a given thing is movable or not is a matter that no legal system can affect—a chair is always capable of being moved in fact; a piece of land is physically always immovable. But a legal system may, for its own purposes, treat that which physically is immovable as movable and *vice versa*. For instance, in English law, the owner of the key of a house is regarded as having an interest in land and, in Austria, wild animals in a forest are treated as immovable; conversely, in Germany, certain types of building are considered movables. The present concern is with that which a legal system may regard as movable or immovable: the literal connotation of those words, as such, is irrelevant.

It may happen that the subject-matter of the dispute is regarded by one of the systems of law with which it is connected as immovable, but by another as movable. The problem then arises, By which legal system is its nature to be decided? In English private international law, that is for the *lex situs*, the law of the place where the property is situate. This is only common sense. Since the courts of the *situs* would of necessity exercise effective ultimate control over the subject-matter, an English court must adopt the same classification as would those courts, if they were dealing with the matter. Hence, in an English court, the question whether, e.g., a certain building in Germany is movable or immovable, will be answered by German law.

In English domestic law itself, property interests are classified as realty or personalty, a division of which the explanation lies in the history of English legal procedure, into which it is unnecessary here to enter. Briefly, freehold interests in land are realty and all other forms of property interest—leaseholds, mortgages, etc., no less than rights in goods, chattels, stocks, shares and suchlike—are personalty. It follows from the preceding paragraphs that this classification is initially abandoned by English courts in a private international law case, in favour of the classification into immovables and movables. For this, there are very good reasons. First, only states with a common law system like England's use the concepts of realty and personalty, so that this classification would be useless in dealing with, e.g., something situate in France. Secondly, it is, strictly, a classification not of things but of interests in things. Land as such is immovable; but one's interest in land may be real or personal. Accordingly, though regarded as personal property in English municipal law, such interests as leaseholds, mortgages, etc., of English land are, in private international law, interests in immovables.

This does not, however, mean that the peculiar English classification has no place in a private international law case. If the subject-matter of the dispute be situate in England and by English law (the *lex situs*) is treated as immovable, it then becomes necessary to know whether the proprietary interest in question is real or personal. Thus, in a dispute over a lease of English land, it would be necessary to know that a leasehold is personal property. The common law distinction will, in short, be important when English law is the *lex situs.*[1]

To illustrate the English approach to property questions in private international law, we may take a simplified version of the facts in *Re Berchtold,*[2] the leading authority on the subject. X died in 1920, intestate, domiciled in Hungary, entitled to leaseholds in England, and the question arose, Who was to succeed him in the property? The court held that, as the subject-matter of X's interest was land in England, English law governed as the *lex situs*, all English land being immovable. But, at the time, English law had different rules for succession on intestacy for realty and for personalty. As X's interest was leasehold, it was personalty, and therefore the person entitled to succeed X was not his heir but the person who, by English law, was regarded as X's next-of-kin. The difference between the distinction of immovables and movables and realty and personalty may here be seen. The first problem is, What is the thing? Subsequently, it may be necessary to consider the nature of the interest in that subjeot-matter.

B. Immovables

English private international law refers all questions concerning the creation, transfer, extent and extinction of proprietary interests in immovables to the *lex situs*. The reason, already adverted to, is the effective control over the subject-matter exercisable by the courts of the *situs*. It would be useless for an English court to decide that X was entitled to a piece of land in France if, in the eyes of French law, Y was the person to whom it belonged. The English judgment would be quite nugatory, for X would be unable to enforce it and get possession of the land in France. 'As regards interests in immovables, it is logical and indeed inevitable that a court sitting in a country other than that of the *situs* should acquiesce in whatever the *forum rei sitae* has decided or would decide.'[3]

This in turn raises the question, what is meant by the *lex situs*

[1] The unfortunate wording of the Wills Act 1861 makes the distinction between realty and personalty important also in connection with the formal validity of wills: see Chapter Five post.

[2] [1923] 1 Ch. 192

[3] Falconbridge, *Essays in Conflict of Laws.*

in this connection? If the court seised of the action must give a decision such as would be given by the courts of the *situs*, then clearly the *lex situs* must mean that law which would be applied by the court of the *situs* in the circumstances of the particular case—not necessarily the municipal law of the *situs*. If, for instance, by Ruritanian law, questions concerning land in Ruritania owned by foreigners were to be governed by the national law of the landowner, then, in any case in England about land in Ruritania owned by a Frenchman, the issue would be determined by French law. For only thus could an English court give the same decision as would be given if the case were litigated in Ruritania. Certainly, where England is the *situs* of the immovables in question, the municipal law of England governs the matter: when the property is situated abroad, though, the law applicable is whatever system the courts of the *situs* would apply in that case.

As previously indicated, the present chapter is concerned with transactions *inter vivos* affecting property rights—gifts, conveyances, etc. At some stage in such cases there is usually a contractual relationship between the parties; indeed, the actual transfer itself may be contractual. The obvious instance is the sale of land in English law: there will be a prior contract between A and B that A will let B have Blackacre for £x and, subsequently, the execution of a formal deed of conveyance—a solemn contract to which both A and B are parties—which, of itself, vests the legal title to Blackacre in B. For the present consideration, it is essential to distinguish the contractual aspect of a transfer from its actual dispositive effect. As a contract, it may have its own proper law, chosen by the parties in accordance with the principles discussed in Chapter Three. Its efficacy as a transfer, however, is in all respects regulated by the *lex situs*. It is this that is meant when it is said that the *lex situs* governs the transfer of immovables. To take again the example of the sale of English land: there would be, in principle, nothing to prevent A and B from selecting some system of law other than that of England to govern their contract; they might even purport to submit the deed of conveyance to, say, German law: but whether that deed actually was effective to transfer Blackacre from A to B would be exclusively determined by English law.

The *lex situs*, in this way, controls all aspects of the actual transfer. Thus, capacity to transfer an interest in immovables is governed by the *lex situs*: in *Bank of Africa v. Cohen*,[1] consequently, the Court of Appeal held that, as she had not complied with the requirements of Roman-Dutch law, which was operative in South Africa where her land was situate, a woman was incapable of creating a valid mortgage over the land. So also for the formalities of a conveyance. In *Adams v. Clutterbuck*,[2] it was held that an informal lease granted in England of sporting rights over Scottish land was valid—by English law, such a lease should have been created by deed under seal but that formality was unnecessary in Scots law which, as the *lex situs*, governed the question. It goes without saying that the essential validity of an alienation would be governed by the *lex situs*: it would, for instance, be impossible to create interests in succession in French land, for such interests are forbidden in French law.

So great indeed is the respect of English courts for the exclusive competence of the *situs* in questions concerning immovables, that, as a general rule, they will refuse to entertain a suit affecting title to or possession of foreign land. This principle emerges from *British South Africa Company v. Companhia de Moçambique*,[3] in which, it will be remembered, the House of Lords held that English courts had no jurisdiction to hear a suit for trespass to land in South Africa. Hence a claim by X, say, that he is entitled to land in Austria would not be heard in English courts, which would hold that only the courts of Austria are competent to deal with X's claim.

To this general rule, however, there are certain exceptions. In the first place, by reason of the international character of maritime law, English courts may hear a claim in respect of damage done by a ship to foreign land. In *The Tolten*,[4] the facts were that the ship, *Tolten*, while leaving Lagos harbour, collided with and damaged a wharf belonging to the plaintiffs. Under maritime law, that gave the plaintiffs a right, enforceable against the ship itself, to seek redress for the damage they suffered.

[1] [1909] 2 Ch. 129
[2] (1883) 10 Q.B.D. 403
[3] [1893] A.C. 602
[4] [1946] P. 135

When the ship put into Liverpool, they commenced the present action and the Court of Appeal held that the claim could be dealt with, even though it was brought in respect of damage to foreign land.

Again, English courts have jurisdiction to make a decision affecting title to foreign immovables, if the question arises in an action for the administration of property under a will (or on intestacy) which is properly before the court. Suppose, for example, that X dies domiciled and resident in England, leaving a will whereby he disposes of property in England and, say, land in France or Germany: if any question arose on the construction of the will, an English court would determine the problem in respect of the whole property, both English and foreign. Thus, in *Re Duke of Wellington*,[1] the question of the devolution of the Spanish estates of the sixth Duke was resolved by the Court of Appeal. It is obviously convenient that this should be so. It would be over-scrupulous for an English court to say, in effect, to the executors, 'We will tell you how to deal with the English property; but, if you want to know how to dispose of the deceased's foreign land, you will have to instruct lawyers in, and get the question answered in the courts of, the country where the land is situate.' The whole problem, after all, arises on an English succession. Of course, though, having taken urisdiction in these circumstances, the English court would certainly invoke the *lex situs* to govern the actual decision so far as it affected foreign land.

Subject to these exceptions, English courts have no jurisdiction in suits involving title to, or possession of, foreign land.[2]

[1] [1948] Ch. 118

[2] The so-called 'equitable jurisdiction' of English courts is frequently cited as another exception. The development within the framework of English law of those principles, rules and remedies which are together styled 'equitable' is a feature of English legal history which it would be out of place to investigate in this book. Accordingly, the particulars of equitable jurisdiction are not discussed: for them, the reader is referred to a larger work, e.g., Dicey, *Conflict of Laws* (6th ed.) 145–148, Cheshire, *Private International Law* (4th ed.) 571–581. By way of general comment, however, it may be said that the equitable jurisdiction is not, strictly speaking, an exception to the general rule as to jurisdiction over immovables. Equitable rights and duties are personal—the jurisdiction is a jurisdiction *in personam* and its exercise is consequently governed by the normal principles of personal jurisdiction discussed in Chapter One ante.

C. Movables

In this section, it is proposed to consider the law relating to particular transfers of movables *inter vivos*, e.g., the sale of a specific chattel—a motor-car or a fur coat; the assignment of a particular debt, etc. General assignments, whereby the whole of an individual's property may be affected, have been already exemplified in the discussion of matrimonial property and will be met again in bankruptcy. Movables may be subclassified as either tangible (goods and chattels—things that can be actually touched) or intangible (stocks, shares, debts, patents, goodwill of businesses, etc.). In the law, tangible movables are designated 'choses in possession' and intangibles 'choses in action'; these terms will be used in the following discussion.

(*i*) *Choses in Possession*

As was the case in the discussion of immovables, the present concern is the dispositive effect of transfers of chattels. Certainly, a sale of a horse, for example, predicates a contract between the vendor and purchaser: but the prime characteristic of a valid sale is the transfer of ownership of the horse from the vendor to the purchaser. Accordingly, our inquiry is directed to ascertaining by which legal system, in a foreign element case, the validity of a purported transfer of title to goods will be determined.

On this subject, it must be admitted, the rule of English law is not clear beyond dispute. There occur, for instance, in older cases, *dicta* to the effect that the *lex domicilii* of the transferor governs the question, a suggestion derived from the old maxim, *mobilia personam sequuntur* (movables follow the person of their owner). It is, however, generally conceded that such a rule can have no place in the modern world in particular transfers. It would be intolerable if X, buying a car from Y in Madeira, while both are on holiday there, had to ascertain where Y is domiciled in order to know what rights he acquired under the contract. As a rule for general assignments, though, this principle has obvious merits of simplicity; hence its importance in connection with the property relations of married persons and in succession.

Again, through the fastening of attention on the contractual form of the usual alienation of goods *inter vivos*, it is, by some, contended that the *lex actus* of the transaction governs the question, the *lex actus* being the proper law of the contract between the parties. Thus, if A agrees to sell B a car which is in a garage in Germany, by a contract which is expressly stated to be governed by French law, on this view French law would determine whether B is now owner of the car. A variant of this view is the theory that the *lex loci actus* governs the disposition of title: using the last example again, if the contract of A and B were made in Italy, Italian law would decide whether it operated to transfer ownership from A to B. Expressions of opinion to support all these views may be found in the law reports.

The dominant English theory, however, and that which alone really receives direct support from decided cases, is that, as with immovables, it is the *lex situs* which determines the issue. On principle, in the first place, it is thought that this is clearly the sound view for the same reason as in the case of immovables—the patently effective control of the *lex situs* over the goods. In English law, the mere making of a contract to sell has the effect of vesting title to the goods in the buyer (in most cases); but in German law title does not pass until the goods are actually delivered to the buyer. Suppose that, by a contract expressly subjected to English law, A in France agrees to sell B certain sacks of sugar stored in a Bonn warehouse: it would surely be pointless for B to proclaim himself owner of the sugar until he has taken possession of it, for in Germany he would not be regarded as owner. If, for instance, he were to resell in France to C, who then goes to Bonn to collect the sugar, C would find that his claim is not recognized.

Turning to authority, the strongest decision in favour of the *lex situs* is probably *Cammell v. Sewell*.[1] There, the Russian agent of an Englishman resident in England loaded a cargo on a German ship at a Russian port, consigned to his English principal at Hull. The ship was wrecked off the coast of Norway but the cargo was safely put ashore. It could have been re-shipped to England but the captain instead sold the cargo to a person who bought it in perfect good faith. The purchaser resold in Norway to the present defendant who sent the cargo to England, where it was now claimed from him by the representatives of the

[1] (1860) 5 H. & N. 728

original consignee. It appeared that by Norwegian law the captain of a ship, in circumstances such as those which had occurred here, had the power to sell the cargo so as to give a good title to a purchaser in good faith, although he would be liable to the original owner if he so sold without justification. The action was dismissed, the Court of Exchequer Chamber holding that the defendant had acquired a good title under Norwegian law. Cockburn C.J. expressly said, 'Although the goods in question were at one time the property of English owners, the property in them was transferred to others by a sale valid according to the law of Norway a country in which the goods were at the time of such sale.' Similarly, in *Re Korvine's Trusts*,[1] the validity of a gift made by a domiciled Russian in England of goods situate in England was governed by English law.

It is therefore considered that, though not perhaps entirely beyond dispute, the English rule is that the validity of a disposition of a chose in possession is governed by the *lex situs* of the goods at the time of the transaction. This of course predicates that the goods have a *situs*; which can scarcely be said to be the case when they are in transit. What then of a sale by A to B in London of, say, a cargo of wheat then being shipped across the Atlantic?; or of a bag of diamonds which, at the time, are being flown from Amsterdam to London? The potential difficulties of such cases are mitigated by the practice of treating the documents of title to the goods as the goods themselves. Thus in the case of goods carried by sea, the bill of lading—a document acknowledging the shipment of the goods, made by or on behalf of the carrier, and containing the terms upon which they are to be carried—represents the goods, so that the cargo will be deemed to be situate wherever the copy despatched to the consignee may be—normally, his place of business. That is to say, the *lex situs* of the bill of lading is also that of the goods. It is possible, however, that there should be a purported disposition of goods in transit, for which no documents of title have been issued: e.g., suppose that X in Paris sells to Y a painting which, at the time of sale, is still in transit from the artist in England. In such exceptional cases, it is thought, the efficacy of the transaction should be determined by the proper law of the agreement between

[1] [1921] 1 Ch. 343

the parties—the *lex actus*—ascertained in accord with the normal principles of contract. The necessity for such special provision for special cases does not, however, abrogate the general rule that, where the goods have a determinable *situs*, the law of that *situs* governs all questions concerning their disposition.

It also follows from the general rule that, in the event of competing claims to the goods, the priority of those claims is determined by the *lex situs* of the goods. *Inglis v. Robertson*,[1] for instance, arose in the following circumstances. A, domiciled in England, owned whisky stored in a Glasgow warehouse, in respect of which he held delivery warrants issued by the warehouseman. To secure a loan from another Englishman, B, A in England indorsed the warrants to B, giving him power to sell the whisky. B did not notify the warehouseman of this transaction and C, Scottish creditors of A, seized the whisky in the warehouse in a manner permitted by Scots law. The action was to determine who had the better title to the whisky, B or C. By English law, A had made a valid assignment of the delivery warrants to B; but, by Scots law, it appeared, it was necessary that B should give notice to the warehouseman in order to perfect his title. As he had not done so, the House of Lords held, by the application of Scots law, that the claim of C was superior to that of B.

(*ii*) *Choses in Action*

Here it is proposed to consider the law relating to *inter vivos* assignments of debts. Negotiable instruments have been already discussed. In general, such other items as shares, copyrights, patents, etc., are regulated by the law of the state in which they are created. Hence, for example, an assignment anywhere of an English patent would have to comply with the Patents and Designs Acts 1907–1946 to be valid in England; the transfer of shares in a company would have to satisfy the law of the state in which the company is incorporated, etc. Such is the broad principle but there is much legislation on these topics, discussion of which is beyond the scope of this book.

At the outset, it may be mentioned that, as will be seen, certain aspects of assignments of debts are referred to the

[1] [1898] A.C. 616

so-called *lex situs* of the debt. Logically, of course, there is a difficulty in ascribing a *situs* to a debt, since it has no physical existence. However, it has become established, as a matter of convenience, to describe as the *situs* of a debt, the place where payment is enforceable.[1] In English private international law, payment is due at the place of the debtor's residence, for the very sound reason that there one can be sure of finding him and so of exacting one's due. Hence, if, under a contract made in Spain between A and B, who resides in Switzerland, B has to pay £100, Swiss law is the *lex situs* of the debt.

The first question which arises in connection with the assignment of debts is, What law determines whether the debt is assignable? Suppose that X and Y make a contract governed by French law, whereby Y who lives in Italy is liable to X for £2,000; X in Germany purports to assign to Z the right to the £2,000: by what law is it to be decided whether the right is so assignable? There is, in fact, no direct English authority on this point but the general consensus of opinion is that the matter is governed by the proper law of the transaction from which the debt arises. Thus, in the example put, French law would decide the question. Similarly, suppose that a retired English civil servant purported to assign in France his pension rights to L; the transaction would be invalid because under English law such rights are not assignable.

Assuming the assignability of the debt, it falls to consider the assignment itself. It was seen in dealing with choses in possession and immovables that all questions arising in connection with proprietary rights therein were governed by the *lex situs* of the land or chattel in question. No such simple or single rule may be postulated, though, for assignments of choses in action. Quite apart from academic controversy, there is a variety of opinion among the judges, as may be seen from a consideration of the leading case of *Republica de Guatemala v. Nuñez*.[2]

The facts from which that case arose were as follows. The president of Guatemala, having deposited money at a London bank, later assigned it to his infant bastard son, Nuñez; both were domiciled and resident in Guatemala. The president was

[1] cf. *Jabbour v. Custodian of Israeli Absentee Property* [1954] 1 W.L.R. 139
[2] [1927] 1 K.B. 669

subsequently deposed and imprisoned and, while in prison, was forced to assign the fund to the Republic of Guatemala. Both Nuñez and the Republic now claimed the money from the bank, which—by the process known as 'interpleading'—withdrew from the proceedings and left Nuñez and the Republic to contest title to the fund. The suit revolved around the assignment to Nuñez for, if that was valid, he had priority over the Republic. In English law, the assignment to Nuñez would have been valid; but by Guatemalan law it was ineffective for two reasons—that Nuñez being an infant had no capacity to accept the transfer; and that the document of transfer had not been in the appropriate form.

Though they all agreed that, by reason of Guatemalan law, the assignment to Nuñez was invalid, the four judges concerned in the case had differing reasons. Thus, Greer J. based his decision on the ground that formalities of an assignment are governed by the *lex loci actus*; this assignment therefore was invalid as it did not comply with the requirements of Guatemalan law. In the Court of Appeal, Bankes L.J. appeared to take the view that the question was one of priorities and governed by the *lex domicilii* of the parties, while Lawrence L.J. was of opinion that formalities are governed by the *lex situs* of the debt assigned but capacity by the *lex domicilii* of the person concerned. Scrutton L.J. agreed with Greer J. that formalities are governed by the *lex loci actus* and also held that Nuñez's capacity was governed by Guatemalan law either as the law of the place where the transaction was effected or as his *lex domicilii.*

In the face of such diversity, it is necessary to consider the matter primarily on principle. Assignments may be of various types and—since the subject-matter is intangible—there is not the same cogency in favour of referring all questions to the *lex situs* which is found in the case of immovables and choses in possession. Suppose that X owes Y £1,000: Y may assign the right to claim that sum to Z by what is virtually a contract of sale, e.g., in return for Z's motor-car or for £850 cash; or he may do so as a gift without any reciprocal benefit at all from Z. The first of these transactions is itself a bilateral contract; the second is a unilateral act of liberality by Y to Z: though both voluntary assignments by Y, these transactions would differ in their nature. Again, Y could be deprived, without his consent, of the right to the money from X if, for instance, Z, being a creditor of Y, were permitted by law to claim debts which are due to Y in order to satisfy his own claim against Y. In such case, Z would be able to claim the £1,000 from X without reference to Y: Y's right to the money would be assigned to Z by operation of law. It is clearly not necessary that each type of assignment should be governed by the same rule.

Involuntary assignments, it is clear, are governed by the *lex situs* of the debt in question. Suppose that X, resident in England, owes £1,000 to Y who resides in France and Y owes a similar sum to Z, who lives in Spain. English law would decide whether Z could claim from X the £1,000 which X owes Y; for England, being the place of X's residence, is the *situs* of his debt to Y. In *Swiss Bank Corporation v. Boemische Bank*,[1] the S bank had recovered judgment in England against the B bank, a Czech institution operating exclusively in Prague which had submitted to the jurisdiction of the English court. To satisfy the judgment, the S bank now sought to claim from a London bank £9,000 which that body owed to the B bank. The London bank refused on the ground that it might thereafter be called upon to pay the £9,000 in Czechoslovakia. The present proceedings were then brought by the S bank against the London bank. The Court of Appeal held that the S bank was entitled to have the £9,000; the money was recoverable and therefore situate in England and, by English law, the S bank's claim was justified.

Turning to voluntary assignments, it may be observed that the English authorities all concern unilateral assignments, i.e., transactions whereby one party transfers his right to claim the money from the debtor to the other without receiving, under the same transaction, any benefit in return. In such cases, the prevailing tendency of English private international law is to refer all questions to the *lex loci actus*. This is understandable. The disposition being the act of one person alone, there is less justification for allowing him to select his governing law than in the case of a bilateral arrangement between two bargaining parties. In the latter case, since each party has his own interests to protect, it is likely that the mutually selected law will be an appro-

[1] [1923] 1 K.B. 673

priate system to govern the transaction. That consideration does not apply in a unilateral assignment—the assignor's choice could be mere caprice. A more certain criterion is desirable; and the law of the place where the transaction is effected would seem to give that criterion.

On the subject of capacity, it is true, Scrutton L.J. opined in *Nuñez's* case that Nuñez's capacity was governed by Guatemalan law as either the *lex loci actus* or the *lex domicilii*. Again, in *Lee v. Abdy*[1] where an assignment by A, domiciled in Cape Province, South Africa, to his wife of the benefit of a life assurance policy was held invalid on the ground that, by the law of the Province, gifts between husband and wife were not allowed, the *lex loci actus* and the *lex domicilii* were identical. The requirements of commercial convenience, however, adverted to in connection with contract, suggest that the decisions should be regarded as based upon the incapacity of the parties under the law of the place where the assignment was made.

The bulk of judicial opinion favours the proposition that compliance with the *lex loci actus* will make the assignment formally valid. Both Greer J. and Scrutton L.J. took that view in *Nuñez's* case and Scrutton L.J.'s opinion was expressly adopted by Maugham J. in *Re Anziani*.[2] Accordingly, it is clear that, if an assignment were made in Germany in the form appropriate under German law, it would be held formally valid in an English court.

Re Anziani is a direct authority that the substantial validity of an assignment is governed by the *lex loci actus*. In that case, a woman purported in Italy to assign a sum of money held on trust for her in England. By Italian law, special formalities were necessary for the execution of a gift and were regarded as a matter of essential validity and not merely as formal requirements in that law. These formalities had not been complied with in the present case and Maugham J., on that ground, held the assignment invalid: Italian law, as the law of the place of the assignment, governed the substance of the transaction.

There is no direct authority relating to truly contractual assignments, e.g., the instance used earlier, where Y assigns to Z

[1] (1886) 17 Q.B.D. 309
[2] [1930] 1 Ch. 407

a debt of £1,000 due from X, in consideration of a motor-car to be delivered by Z to Y. It must be mentioned, though, that, in the cases dealing with unilateral assignments discussed above, the law was stated in terms of assignments generally, not specifically as for unilateral assignments. However, it is thought that, on principle, the same rules should apply to a bilateral assignment as are operative in respect of an ordinary contract. That is to say, the capacity of the parties and the essential validity of the assignment should be governed by its proper law and the assignment should be formally valid if it satisfies either the proper law or the *lex loci actus*. Thus, if the parties to the assignment have expressly chosen a law to govern their transaction, compliance with that law on any question of capacity, substantial validity or formalities should be sufficient to ensure the validity of the assignment in an English court.

When there is no express choice of law—and hitherto there is no instance—then, of course, it falls to consider the presumed intention of the parties. This, it is thought, enables us to appreciate that, as noted, the law in the cases considered earlier was stated with reference to assignments generally. For, in view of the essential simplicity of the transaction and the intangibility of its subject-matter—both being factors which inevitably reduce the number of legal systems with which the assignment could be connected—it would seem perfectly appropriate to presume that the parties have chosen the law of the place where they made their assignment. It is therefore submitted that, in the absence of a choice of law, the proper law of such an assignment will be the *lex loci actus*. Hence, if X in Spain assigned to Y, a domiciled German, a sum of money due to him from A in New York, in return for a loan from Y to enable him to buy shares in a Spanish company, Spanish law would govern the assignment.

There may be successive assignments of the same debt. For instance, A owes B £1,000; B assigns his claim to C as a gift and C assigns it to D to compromise a legal action that D has commenced against him. Each assignment would, of course, be considered separately in accordance with the principles just discussed, in order to determine its validity as to capacity, form and substance.

No less possible is a succession of assignments by the same

assignor to different assignees: e.g., A is entitled to £1,000 in a London bank account; he assigns it to B as security for a loan from B and later purports to assign it again to C to secure another loan. In such cases, problems of priorities may arise: in the example, suppose that A dies without repaying either B or C —which of the creditors, B or C, is entitled to the London bank account? Each assignment may, in itself, be perfectly valid by the rules stated; but that does not tell us who can claim the fund. The English rule as to priorities cannot be said to be established beyond dispute. In *Kelly v. Selwyn*,[1] X, an Englishman domiciled in New York, assigned in New York to his wife the share to which he was entitled in an English trust fund. By New York law, the assignment was complete and vested title in the wife without the necessity of informing the trustees of the fund that the assignment had taken place and they were in fact not notified. Subsequently, in England, X purported to re-assign the share to Y as security for a loan and Y did inform the trustees that the share had been assigned to him. In the action, the question was whether the wife or Y had the better title and it was held that Y prevailed. Although the earlier New York transaction had been perfectly good in itself, nevertheless, since in English law the first assignee to notify the debtor takes priority,[2] Y had precedence. This decision could be taken as authority for the proposition that the *lex situs* of the fund assigned governs priorities: it will be seen, however, that in the case English law was also the proper law of the fund—it was an English trust fund. It is thought that this affords an opportunity to frame a more satisfactory rule—namely, that the proper law of the debt assigned governs the question of the priority of competing claims to the debt. This is considered more desirable because a debt may be situated in more than one place, in that it may be claimable in more than one place. For instance, an insurance company with head offices in London may issue a policy at its Paris branch; when the policy becomes payable, the holder may claim at the Paris office—but he could also claim in London. But, wherever it may be claimable, the sum due becomes due under the policy, the proper law of which is the proper law of the debt—and

[1] [1905] 2 Ch. 117
[2] Subject to some qualifications not here in point.

which is single. As providing a simpler and more certain rule, then, it is suggested that *Kelly v. Selwyn* should be regarded as establishing that questions of priorities are determined by the proper law of the debt assigned. Accordingly, in the example cited, English law would decide whether B or C had the better title to the £1,000 in the London bank account.

D. Bankruptcy

In common with other developed systems of law, English law has the institution of bankruptcy. This is a process whereby the property of someone unable to pay his debts is placed in the hands of a public official to be applied, according to fixed priorities, for the satisfaction of his creditors. In due course, the debtor may receive his discharge in bankruptcy, which, as it were, enables him to start life afresh. The whole process is both businesslike and humane: it allows all creditors to get something of what is due to them from the debtor, while also enabling the debtor to obtain some relief from what may be a crushing burden of debt. In England, the official who administers the debtor's assets is called a 'trustee in bankruptcy' and the term, 'trustee', will be used generally in this section to designate any person or persons who exercise similar functions in other systems of law.

English law relating to bankruptcy is contained in the Bankruptcy Act 1914 (as amended by an Act of 1926), hereafter called simply 'the Act'. To become bankrupt in England, a person must both be a 'debtor' and have committed what is called an 'act of bankruptcy', as defined by the Act. A debtor is a person who, at the time of committing an act of bankruptcy, was present or resident in England or carrying on business—alone, in partnership, or through an agent—in England. His nationality and domicile are, as such, irrelevant. Section 1 (1) of the Act gives a lengthy list of the circumstances which constitute an act of bankruptcy. It is not within the scope of this book to repeat it: suffice it to say that the essence of acts of bankruptcy is an indication by the debtor of inability or unwillingness to honour his debts and that some of the acts need not be committed in England—e.g., a gift or other transfer, in England or elsewhere, of property made in order to defraud creditors. Where these conditions are fulfilled, a debtor may present his own petition in bankruptcy.

As often as not, however, it is not the debtor but his creditors who seek his bankruptcy. Now, on the definition of a debtor, simply as it stands above, it would be possible to make bankrupt in England a Frenchman, say, who happened to commit an act of bankruptcy while on holiday in this country, even though his real residence and substantial business interests were all abroad. That, however, was not the intention of the Act, which is really concerned to ensure that proceedings could be taken in respect of persons who are, in a real sense, subject to English jurisdiction through residence, ordinary or commercial.[1] Accordingly, before a creditor can present a petition for the bankruptcy of a debtor, further stipulations, set out in s. 4 (1) of the Act, must be complied with. The debt due to the petitioner must be a sum certain of at least £50, the act of bankruptcy must have occurred within three months before the petition, and the debtor must be domiciled in England or else—within a year before the petition—have had a dwellinghouse there or carried on business in England, alone, in partnership or through an agent.

Suppose, therefore, that X, domiciled and resident in Hungary, borrowed £2,000 from Y, an Englishman, in Paris and then, six months ago, while on holiday in England, transferred his London bank account to his wife. X could now present a petition himself in the English court but Y would not be able to seek X's bankruptcy here. The difference of treatment of debtor's and creditor's petitions is understandable: it is essentially a particular manifestation of the jurisdictional principles of submission and effectiveness considered in Chapter One.

When a person is adjudicated bankrupt in England, s. 38 of the Act purports to vest in his trustee all his property, immovable as well as movable, wherever situate and of whatever kind. Bankruptcy in English law, therefore, operates as a universal assignment of the debtor's property; the principle of s. 38 is indeed described as the principle of universality. As a statute of the Westminster Parliament, the Act can vest in the trustee title

[1] Until the Bankruptcy Act of 1913, indeed, the law of bankruptcy applied only to British subjects or to foreigners resident in England and thus owing allegiance to the British Crown.

to any property in the Empire; but whether it has the same effect on property situate elsewhere will in fact, of necessity, depend upon the *lex situs*. Certainly, an English court would consider the trustee entitled to, say, land of his bankrupt in France; and s. 22 of the Act does provide that the bankrupt must do all in his power to ensure the transfer to his trustee of all his assets, wherever situate. But whether the trustee could in fact obtain control of the land by virtue of his English title alone would depend on whether French law conceded the universal effect of the English bankruptcy—a British statute, as such, cannot affect property in France.

It has been said that the object of bankruptcy is to make the debtor's assets available to satisfy his creditors. And, regardless who presents the petition, all creditors are entitled to claim in the bankruptcy, whether their debt was contracted in England or elsewhere or under English law or not. Questions of priority may thus arise between competing claims. Such questions and all matters generally which concern the problem whether a debt may be proved, are determined by English law. That relates, of course, to the *admissibility* of the debt; the *existence* of the debt is determined by the law under which it is alleged to have been contracted. Suppose that X made a contract with Y in Paris, expressly stated to be governed by French law, under which X became indebted to Y for £1,000; Y himself later became indebted to X for £50: X now is adjudicated bankrupt in England and Y wishes to claim in the bankruptcy. French law will determine whether the contract was valid and thus whether X did contract a debt of £1,000 to Y: English law, as the *lex fori* of the bankruptcy, will decide whether the claim is admissible and whether the £50 may be set off against Y's claim so reducing it, in effect, to £950. In the same way, when the estate is settled up, all creditors are entitled to the same dividend out of the bankrupt's assets and their right to receive a dividend is governed by English law, the law of the bankruptcy.

Bankruptcy is not a permanent status: the person adjudicated bankrupt comes under certain disabilities, e.g., he may not obtain credit for more than £10 without disclosing his status, etc. But, in due course, he may petition for his discharge from bankruptcy; and, if granted, the discharge operates in English law as a complete extinction of all save a very few of his previous obligations. Even, for instance, if his creditors received only six shillings in the pound of what they were owed, he will be quite free from claims by them: on discharge, the bankrupt starts afresh with a clean slate.

The rules operative when English bankruptcy jurisdiction is in fact exercised have here been discussed. It must be noted, though, that the jurisdiction is discretionary: the presentation of a petition will not necessarily be followed by the adjudication of the debtor as a bankrupt. The Act, the Bankruptcy (Scotland) Act 1913 and the Bankruptcy and Insolvency (Ireland) Act 1857, ensure that a bankruptcy in any of the home countries has exclusive force in other parts of the United Kingdom. For the rest, it is true that a foreign adjudication would not of itself prevent English proceedings—the attitude of English courts is summed up in the words of Fry L.J., 'I think a receiving order (i.e., in England) ought to be pronounced where the conditions of the Act have been satisfied, unless there be some valid reason to the contrary.'[1] But such a reason might be the fact of an adjudication in a foreign state where the bulk of the debtor's assets are situated: cf. *In re Robinson*.[2]

English courts recognize in a foreign adjudication the same universality of effect which characterizes an English one, subject to certain qualifications. In the first place, if, by the law of the state in which he is appointed, the foreign trustee becomes entitled only to property of the debtor in that state (as is the general rule in the United States),[3] then his recognition in England would be limited to the same extent. This is only sensible; it would be excessive liberality to accord to the foreign trustee greater authority than is granted him in the state of his appointment. Again, a distinction must be taken between the movable and immovable property of the bankrupt. So far as immovables are concerned, England could recognize his title only in so far as it is conceded by the *lex situs*: certainly, so far as English land is concerned, English law—liberal though it is in the recognition

[1] *Re Artola Hermanos* (1890) 24 Q.B.D. 640
[2] (1883) 22 Ch.D. 816
[3] In the U.S.A., however, bankruptcy is essentially a federal matter so that private international law problems between states are not common.

of foreign bankruptcy provisions—would not acknowledge the foreign appointment as vesting title in the trustee. Similarly, French law would decide whether the trustee of a person made bankrupt in Spain was entitled to the debtor's French land. But, subject to these provisos, English law does recognize the universality of a foreign adjudication. Hence, English courts would recognize the title of, say, the Dutch trustee of a person made bankrupt in Holland to the debtor's bank account in England.

Again, with reference to foreign bankruptcies, the English rule is that all questions concerning whether a creditor's debt is provable, the priority of debts, etc., are governed by the law of the adjudicating state; that is to say, as in the case of an English bankruptcy, the *lex fori* governs the questions—though, again, the actual existence of the debt would be determined by the law of the transaction from which it arose. Hence, if a person claiming to be a creditor of a French bankrupt, under a contract governed by Dutch law, sought to establish in an English court against the French trustee that he had a claim in the administration, the existence of the debt would be decided by Dutch law, while the admissibility of the claim would fall to French law.

From the circumstances in which English law itself claims bankruptcy jurisdiction, it is obvious that England does not accept the principle, which has from time to time been urged, that the courts of a debtor's domicile should have exclusive jurisdiction. Similarly, as a person may have assets in more than one state, English law takes the view that the mere fact of proceedings in bankruptcy in one state does not prevent their initiation in another state also. In short, English courts do not recognize any principle of unity in bankruptcy proceedings. A debtor may be made bankrupt in more places than one, whether including England or not, at one time.

Since England, while thus accepting the possibility of concurrent bankruptcies, also acknowledges—subject to the provisos noted—the universality in effect of any adjudication, considerable difficulties may arise through competing claims of rival trustees to the same property. Suppose that X is made bankrupt in Holland, by whose law the trustee is, as in English law, entitled to all his debtor's property; and that subsequently bankruptcy proceedings are also commenced in England: X had property in England, both movable and immovable, and the question now arises whether the English or the Dutch trustee is entitled thereto. On the principles considered above, since the Dutch adjudication could not affect the English immovables, the English trustee would be entitled to the English land. But, as England recognizes the universal effect of bankruptcy on movables, the English movables would have become vested in the Dutch trustee upon his appointment, and so would no longer be available—as the debtor's property—when the English trustee was appointed: the Dutchman would be entitled.

In the same way, if there is no English order but there are competing foreign trustees claiming assets in England of a person made bankrupt in two or more foreign countries, an English court would recognize the title of the first one appointed, so far as movables are concerned. It is also thought that, in the exercise of its discretion, the court should allow the first trustee to have been appointed to realize any immovable property of the bankrupt in England. Hence, if X were adjudicated bankrupt in Holland and subsequently also in France, his Dutch trustee would be entitled to his movables in England; probably, he would also be allowed to dispose of any English land belonging to X.

There remains the question of a foreign discharge in bankruptcy. As seen, an English discharge under the Act completely erases the old debts of the bankrupt and is recognized as having this effect throughout British territories; a similar effect for Scottish and Northern Ireland discharges is provided by the Acts of 1913 and 1857 mentioned earlier. The effect of a foreign discharge, however, will depend, in the first place, upon whether it is intended, by the law under which it is granted, to operate as a complete discharge from old debts. If it did not, then it would not be recognized as extinguishing the debt in England. Suppose that X was adjudicated bankrupt in Arcadia and his creditors received ten shillings in the pound; later he was discharged in Arcadia but, by Arcadian law, creditors may sue a discharged bankrupt for the unsatisfied portion of their claims. Y, to whom X owed £1,000 at the time of his bankruptcy, could sue X in England for the balance of £500 and the Arcadian discharge would be no defence to the action.

Where a foreign discharge is intended, by the law under which it is granted, to extinguish former liabilities of the bankrupt, it will be recognized in England only if it be granted under the proper law of the liability in question.[1] A contractual debt, for instance, will be considered to be released only if the discharge be granted under the proper law of the contract from which the debt arose. Suppose therefore that X owed Y £1,000 under a contract governed by French law: X is adjudicated bankrupt in Germany, his creditors getting ten shillings in the pound dividend, and is later granted a discharge in Germany: Y would be able to sue for the remaining £500 in an action in England and it would be no defence for X to plead his German discharge. The principle is a simple one—the obligation having been incurred under a particular law can be discharged only under that law. In this respect, however, there is a divergence between English law and the effect which English courts accord to foreign laws, in the matter of discharge in bankruptcy: for, of course, an English discharge would be a good answer to a claim for the balance of any debt which is deemed to be satisfied in the bankruptcy, whatever the proper law of that debt.

[1] *Ellis v. McHenry* (1871) L.R. 6 C.P. 228, 234
Gibbs v. Soc. Ind. et Comm. des Métaux (1890) 25 Q.B.D. 399

CHAPTER FIVE

LAW OF SUCCESSION

UPON the death of a person, it becomes necessary to wind up his affairs—to pay off debts unpaid by him at his death, collect debts which were due to him, etc.—and thereafter to ensure that the net assets of his estate are transmitted to those legally entitled to them, whether such persons be designated by the deceased in a will or determined by rules of law in the absence of any will. These questions are the subject-matter of the law of succession. The process of winding up is described as 'administration', the disposition of the assets upon completion of the administration is a matter of 'distribution' of the estate.

Generally, in continental systems of law which derive from Roman law, whether a person dies testate or intestate (i.e., whether having made a will or not), all his property passes into the hands of his heirs or universal legatees, who thereupon become responsible for both administration and distribution of the estate. In Roman law, the heir or heirs—for there could be more than one heir—stepped into the shoes of the deceased, as it were, becoming liable to settle up the estate. Similarly, in its modern continental descendants, the heirs or universal legatees (for again there may be more than one), becoming entitled to the deceased's property, also become liable to pay off his debts, etc., and then to dispose of the residue of the estate according to the directions of the will, if any, or else under the intestate succession rules of the legal system in question.

In English law, however, no one may administer the property of a deceased person without having been granted authority to do so by the Court or the Probate Registry. Persons receiving such authority may be either 'executors' or 'administrators', generically described as 'personal representatives'. If nominated in a will to administer the estate, a person is an executor and obtains from the Court a 'grant of probate'; if the deceased nominated no one or left an invalid will or no will at all, then certain persons[1] may take out 'letters of administration' and are known as administrators.

It is the function of the personal representatives, of whichever sort, to settle up the estate of the deceased and then to distribute in accordance with the terms of the will if any, or else according to the appropriate rules governing intestate succession. It may be mentioned that the nominated executor is not unknown in continental systems of law, but his functions are generally supervisory of the heir or heirs—the heirs do the actual administering; the executor, if any, sees that the heirs perform their tasks properly: whereas, as we have seen, in England the personal representatives actually administer. Again, while in England the property of the deceased vests in the personal representatives as owners, it is in the heirs that the estate vests on the continent, even where there is an executor: the continental heir, in short, from an English viewpoint, combines the functions of both personal representative and residuary beneficiary.

In view of this difference between English and continental practice, it is clear that problems of private international law may arise in connection with both administration and distribution. A person governed by a continental system may die leaving property in England, for instance, where the authority of the Court is required to deal with the property of the dead. Again, an English personal representative may find that he has to consider the rules of a foreign system of law in distributing to beneficiaries, because, e.g., succession to movables is governed by the *lex domicilii* of the deceased at death.

It is therefore proposed to consider first the question of administration and then that of distribution, distinguishing in the latter between intestate and testate succession.

A. Administration

The English court has jurisdiction, under section 2 (1) of the Administration of Justice Act 1932, to make a grant of probate or of administration in respect of a deceased person, even though he or she left no estate. It is, however, probable that a grant will be made only if the deceased died domiciled in England or if

[1] A list in order of entitlement is contained in the Non-Contentious Probate Rules 1954, rules 19, 21, 26.

there be some property of the deceased—or in the administration of which he was concerned, e.g., as trustee—in England. In such a case, a grant will be made even though part of the estate be situate outside this country.[1] Indeed, in respect of assets in England, it is essential that a grant of probate or administration be obtained, even though the succession generally be governed by some other system of law. Otherwise, a person dealing with the deceased's property in England would be treated as an 'executor de son tort', which means that he would be liable to be sued by the person properly entitled to be personal representative and made liable for death duties, etc.: also unsuspecting debtors of the estate who pay an executor de son tort will find that they have not discharged their obligations: *New York Breweries v. A.G.*[2]

It is now necessary to consider who is entitled to an English grant in respect of property in England, when the succession is governed by some other legal system, especially one based upon the general continental pattern. As administration is a matter of procedure,[3] it is governed by the *lex fori* and thus the English court would not be obliged to follow the foreign law in question and grant authority to the person entitled thereunder. In fact, though, it is the practice of the English court to grant administration—if he applies for it—to the person who has, under the *lex domicilii* of the deceased, to perform the duties which an English personal representative would discharge. Such person may be a universal legatee or heir, in the continental sense—the name does not matter so long as he is the person performing the functions.[4] That is the general rule: but if there were some good reason for not following the *lex domicilii*—as, e.g., if the foreign administrator were an infant or bankrupt—the English court would follow a different course.

If the foreign administrator does not apply or is rejected, then a grant might be made to anyone qualified to take a grant under the rules of English law, frequently an English creditor

[1] cf. *Re Duke of Wellington* [1948] Ch. 118
[2] [1899] A.C. 62
[3] *Re Wilks* [1935] 1 Ch. 645
[4] See now Practice Direction [1953] 1 W.L.R. 1237–8 and Non-Contentious Probate Rules 1954, rules 29 and 30

of the deceased. Nevertheless, in such case the foreign administrator (known as the 'principal administrator') would still be primarily responsble for the general winding up of the estate. The person who has an English grant would be an 'ancillary administrator', who, after settling up the English affairs of the deceased, might generally transfer the surplus assets to the principal administrator for transmission to the intended beneficiaries. For instance, in *Re Achillopoulos*,[1] a person whose succession was governed by Greek law died leaving property in England. He had numerous heirs who, by Greek law, were responsible for the administration of his property. An English solicitor was authorized to take out administration in England and he, after winding up the English estate, wished to know to whom he might transmit the balance. The Court of Appeal held that it might be transferred to anyone who, under the deceased's personal law, performed the duties which in England devolve upon the personal representative.

In theory, an English grant of probate or administration is unlimited in scope so that, by English law, a personal representative would be entitled to take action in respect of all property of the deceased, wherever situate, including any property brought into this country after the grant has been made. In fact, though, as in the case of an English trustee in bankruptcy, this theoretical omnicompetence can be realized only in so far as the English grant may be recognized by the *lex situs* of the property to which he makes claim. Determining the *situs* of immovables and tangible movable property obviously causes no difficulty; the location of intangible movables, however, depends upon the nature of the property in question. Thus a judgment debt is situate in the country of the court under whose judgment it arises, the goodwill of a business has its *situs* where the business is carried on, etc.; an illuminating discussion may be found in *A.G. v. Bouwens*.[2] Though in theory vested with complete title to the deceased's property, therefore, an English personal representative may find himself obliged to seek authority from the courts of the *situs* of the property in question; for some countries will not recognize the English grant any more than the

[1] [1928] 1 Ch. 433
[2] (1838) 4 M. & W. 171

English court recognizes a foreign title, as universal legatee or heir, to property in England. It is, perhaps, not uninteresting in this connection to note the refusal of control of English assets without an English grant of authority as against the readiness of English courts to admit the title of a foreign trustee in bankruptcy. This difference of attitude towards two not dissimilar functions may perhaps be explained by the absence of the commercial element in the administration of deceased persons' estates.

In the exercise of his duties as personal representative, the English executor or administrator must pay off the debts of the deceased, wheresoever contracted, and then distribute the residue or, if he is an ancillary administrator, usually remit the balance to the principal administrator for distribution. Both English and foreign creditors may claim in the administration on an equal footing, save for certain specially preferred creditors. But, by reason of the procedural character of the administration of estates, all questions of the admissibility of debts, priorities of competing claims, etc., are, as in bankruptcy, governed by English law as the *lex fori*: *Re Kloebe*.[1] Again, though, as in bankruptcy, the validity of the debt would be determined in accordance with the law under which it arose.

This principle is of particular importance when the English administration is ancillary to a foreign winding up. As seen in *Re Achillopoulos*, the general rule is that, after completing the English administration, the English representative remits the balance of assets to the foreign principal for distribution to the beneficiaries. But, if there be foreign creditors whose claims are inadmissible in England, but who could enforce them as against the principal administrator, then the English court will authorize the English administrator to distribute directly to the beneficiaries.

The reason is, of course, that, if the English property were transferred to the foreign principal, he would be liable to satisfy the claims of the creditor who could not realize his claim in England. That the English court should thus be prepared, apparently, to assist in preventing creditors of the deceased from receiving what is owed to them, may seem surprising. The legal justification is that the settlement of claims is a matter of administration and, so far as the English property is concerned, English

[1] (1884) 28 Ch.D. 175

law—which is decisive on the matter—holds that its administration is complete and the time for distribution has arrived. The principle is well illustrated in *Re Lorillard*.[1] In that case, a testator died domiciled in one of the United States, leaving property and creditors in both England and America. Administration was taken out in both relevant jurisdictions. In England, after all creditors had been paid, there was a surplus: in the United States, after all available assets were exhausted, there were still some debts unpaid, which were claimable under the domiciliary law of the deceased but were probably unenforceable in English law. The American personal representatives, as principal administrators, claimed that the English surplus should be remitted to them so that they could satisfy the unpaid American creditors. The Court of Appeal, however, held that these creditors should be given time to prove their claims in England but that, if they were in fact unenforceable in English law, then the English administrator was to distribute the English balance direct to the beneficiaries of the will. Without questioning the legitimate distinction between administration and distribution, however, it may well be wondered whether it is not morally more desirable that all claims against the estate of a deceased person, which may be valid under the law governing his succession, should be satisfied before beneficiaries begin to enjoy his posthumous liberality.

A series of statutory provisions has been enacted to facilitate the mutual recognition of grants of probate or administration within the United Kingdom and other British territories, so avoiding the necessity of separate applications for administration in each country in which there may be property of the deceased. Within the United Kingdom, an English grant in respect of a person dying domiciled in England may be resealed in Northern Ireland or in Scotland and will operate thereafter as though initially granted in Northern Ireland or Scotland, as the case may be; similar provisions apply for the resealing in England of Scottish and Northern Ireland grants.[2] Likewise, the Colonial

[1] [1922] 2 Ch. 638

[2] The relevant statutes are: Northern Ireland (Miscellaneous Provisions) Act 1932, s. 2; Confirmation of Executors Act 1858, s. 14; Supreme Court of Judicature Act 1925, ss. 168, 169; Administration of Justice Act 1928, s. 10

Probates Act 1892 authorizes the resealing in England of grants made in other territories under the British Crown outside the United Kingdom: the operation of the Act in relation to any territory depends upon the making of an Order in Council, which will be made only where the territory in question makes reciprocal arrangements for the resealing of United Kingdom grants.[1]

B. DISTRIBUTION

As previously stated, upon completion of the winding up of an estate, the personal representatives have to distribute the surplus to the appropriate beneficiaries. The discussion of distribution may be subdivided into a consideration of, first, intestate and then testate succession.

1. *Intestate Succession*

The English rule of private international law is that succession to the movable property of a person dying intestate is governed by the *lex domicilii* of the deceased as at the time of his death. That law determines all such questions as, e.g., the persons entitled to benefit, whether they have capacity to take such benefit, the extent to which they shall benefit, etc. It may thus well happen that a person may succeed who, under English municipal law, would be ineligible. For instance, in English law, bastard children have no rights of succession upon the intestate death of their natural father. But, in *Doglioni v. Crispin*,[2] finding that a different rule prevailed in Portuguese law, the House of Lords upheld the claim of the bastard child of a British subject, who died intestate domiciled in Portugal, to movable property of the deceased in England.

The nationality, place of residence, etc., of the intestate at death are, as such, irrelevant to the question of his succession. It may be, though, that he dies domiciled in a state by whose law the succession of foreigners is referred to the national law of the deceased, as, for instance, in German or Italian law. In such case, it will be remembered, the doctrine of *renvoi*, which was

[1] For resealing procedure, see Non-Contentious Probate Rules 1954, rules 40 and 41

[2] (1866) L.R. 1 H.L. 301

discussed in Chapter One, is operative. In other words, the law applicable is that which would be applied in the courts of the domiciliary state if they were seised of an action concerning the succession of the intestate.

It must further be noted that the *lex domicilii* of the intestate determines only questions of actual succession. All systems of law have rules determining who is beneficially entitled upon the death of an intestate; in English law, for example, the matter is regulated by the Administration of Estates Act 1925 and the Intestates' Estates Act 1952. In the absence of other possible claimants, the law usually provides that the property shall vest in the state. This may be done either by purporting to treat the state as ultimate heir or by frankly regarding the property as 'heirless' and vesting it in the state as the general authority of the community concerned, as is the case with *bona vacantia* (ownerless property) in England.

The difference in the basis of the state claim in such cases would appear to be only formal. It is nevertheless of importance when a person dies intestate, without other eligible claimants, leaving movable property in England. If, under the intestate's *lex domicilii*, the domiciliary state is regarded as heir in such cases, its claim would, in an English court, be regarded as one of true succession and therefore to be upheld. If, on the other hand, its claim were based upon a ground similar to that of the Crown under English law, an action by the domiciliary state to assert title to the English movables of the intestate would fail. The property being in such a case heirless under the *lex domicilii*, it will vest in the state of the *situs*, in the person of the Crown, as *bona vacantia*. The reason is that, in such circumstances, the claim of the state of the domicile would not be one of succession but a purported exercise of sovereign authority—which it cannot make in another state.

Thus, in the recent *Re Maldonado*,[1] where a Spaniard died intestate domiciled in Spain, leaving securities on deposit at a London bank, the Spanish state, in the absence of any next-of-kin, claimed administration thereof as being the sole successor under Spanish law. Being satisfied that, in Spanish law, the state is genuinely treated as an heir in such circumstances, the Court of

[1] [1954] 2 W.L.R. 64

Appeal upheld the claim. In the older *Re Barnett's Trusts*,[1] on the other hand, the Austrian state claimed the English property of a person who died domiciled in Austria, on the ground that, by Austrian law, as the intestate died childless, his property would be taken by the state. The action failed; the Austrian provision contemplated state acquisition not as heir but simply by reason of its authority: accordingly, the property vested in the power which was competent to assert such authority in England, i.e., the Crown.

In accord with general principle, all questions of succession to the immovable property of an intestate are governed by the *lex situs* of the property in question. In *Duncan v. Lawson*,[2] a domiciled Scot by his will left certain English leasehold properties to charities. By English law, the charities could not accept the bequest and the deceased accordingly was intestate as to the leaseholds. It was held that they devolved on the persons entitled to succeed under the English Statutes of Distributions. It will be seen that here the *lex situs*, English law, determined the capacity of the intended beneficiaries and also the nature of the property interest in question (personalty) and its actual devolution. In like manner, if a person died domiciled in England and intestate leaving land in Germany and in Scotland, the succession thereto would be governed separately by German and Scots law respectively. It must be noted also that, equally in the case of immovables, *renvoi* would be operative, if necessitated by the provisions of the *lex situs*.

2. *Testate Succession*

The obvious prerequisite of succession under the terms of a will is a valid will, the requirements of which must therefore be considered. Unfortunately, the Wills Act 1861 (usually and hereafter referred to as Lord Kingsdown's Act) makes certain provisions in respect of wills of *personal estate*, thus cutting across—and rendering inappropriate here—the normal private international law division of property into movables and immovables. For this reason, it is necessary to consider together the factors which may affect the validity of a will whether of movable or of immovable property.

[1] [1902] 1 Ch. 847
[2] (1889) 41 Ch.D. 394

(i) Testamentary Capacity

It is clear that, in the first place, the testator must have capacity to make a will; otherwise the document that he leaves after his death will be of no effect. Capacity to make a will of immovables is, as might be expected, governed by the *lex situs* of the property in question: *Re Hernando.*[1] In respect of movables, English private international law looks to the *lex domicilii* of the testator to determine his capacity. Thus, in *In Goods of Maraver,*[2] the court admitted to probate a will affecting movables in England which was made by a married woman domiciled in Spain: at that time, married women, in English law, had no power of testation, but in Spanish law were not so incapacitated.

If, as in the *Maraver* case, the testator is domiciled at all times in the same state, no difficulty arises. Much controversy, though, has centred in the books on the question of a person's having a different domicile at death from that which he possessed when making his will and having testamentary capacity by the law of one state but not by that of the other. In England, for instance, a person under twenty-one is in general incapable of making a will; but, in some legal systems, e.g., that of Germany, testamentary capacity may exist earlier. Suppose that a person domiciled in Germany made a will when sixteen, but died at the age of twenty domiciled in England: would the will be admitted to probate? In short, what *lex domicilii* determines the power to make a will of movables—that at the making of the will or that of the testator at death?

There is no clear authority in the cases and the writers are broadly divided into supporters of the domicile at making and those who favour the domicile at death. In support of the former, it may be urged that, though a will becomes operative only on the death of its maker, nevertheless it must be capable of efficacy from the time of making. On the other hand, it may legitimately be observed that an alleged will must be recognized as valid by the *lex domicilii* of the testator at death since that system governs the general validity of the will. It is thought that both are important—the testator must have capacity by the law of his domicile both when making the will and when it becomes oper-

[1] (1884) 27 Ch.D. 284
[2] (1828) 1 Hagg. Ecc. 498

ative, i.e., at his death. In effect, the will must be capable of being effective from its making; whether it is in fact effective depends upon the law governing the succession. Thus in the example above, the German youth's will would not be valid because he lacked capacity under the law of his domicile at death.

(ii) Formalities

In general, the formal validity of a will of immovable property is governed by the *lex situs*, as is illustrated in *Pépin v. Bruyère*,[1] where a will of English freeholds made in French form by a British subject domiciled in France was held invalid for non-compliance with the Wills Act 1837. Likewise, a will of movables should comply with the formal requirements of the *lex domicilii* at death of the testator.

It was the application of the rule as to movables in *Bremer v. Freeman*,[2] which produced the much criticized Lord Kingsdown's Act. In the case, the Privy Council rejected a will made in English form by an Englishwoman who died domiciled in France; to be effective it should have been made in French form. The consequence was the passing of an Act 'to amend the laws with respect to wills of personal estate made by British subjects', championed by Lord Kingsdown.

Section 1 provides that a will of personalty of a British subject made *outside* the United Kingdom shall be valid as to form if it satisfies the formal requirements of one of the following legal systems:

(a) the law of the place where it was made
(b) the law of the testator's domicile at the time of making the will
(c) the law of the testator's domicile of origin, if that be within the territories of the British Crown.

Section 2 enacts that a will of personalty of a British subject made *within* the United Kingdom shall be formally valid if it complies with the formal requirements of the law of the place where it is made. In so far as they provide that satisfaction of the law of the place where the will is made shall formally validate it, these sections are really adopting the principle met earlier, *locus*

[1] [1900] 2 Ch. 504
[2] (1857) 10 Moo. P.C. 306

regit actum, which is found also in many other systems of law, e.g., German law, in this connection, and which in those systems—through the aid of *renvoi*—would validate many wills which might otherwise be formally ineffective. For instance, suppose a domiciled German makes a will of movables in England in English form: the *lex domicilii*, to which an English court would look, refers formalities of such wills to the law of the place of making, i.e., to English law; so the English court—applying the law which the courts of the domicile would apply if they had to decide the point—itself would test the will by English law and so would uphold it. The particular feature of Lord Kingsdown's Act is that it adopts the principle in respect only of British subjects and of the peculiar common law kind of property, personalty.

As to the persons to whom the sections apply, all subjects of the Crown were simply British subjects in 1861, when the Act was passed. Now, since the British Nationality Act 1948, the Act will apply, of itself,[1] principally to citizens of the United Kingdom and Colonies. A British subject with a Jamaican domicile of origin, but domiciled in Spain at the time that he makes a will in Italy while on holiday in that country, could draft his will in the form appropriate under Spanish or Italian or Jamaican law; and it would, by virtue of Section 1, be formally valid even if he dies domiciled in France. Likewise, if a British subject domiciled in England made a will in Scotland in Scots form, the will would be preserved under Section 2 although he died still domiciled in England. It must, though, be noted that the sections provide alternatives to, not substitutes for, the common law rules. A will of movables, for instance, which did satisfy the formal requirements of the testator's domicile at death would be valid without recourse to the Act.

As the sections refer to personalty and not to movables simply, wills of such interests in English land as leaseholds, mortgages, etc., may be formally validated under the provisions of Lord Kingsdown's Act. In *Re Grassi*,[2] for example, a naturalized British subject of Italian origin, while visiting Italy, made a will in Italian form, whereby he purported to dispose of English

[1] In the Dominions, e.g., in Canada, there are local forms of the Act.
[2] [1905] 1 Ch. 584

leaseholds: the will was admitted to probate. Similarly, where a British subject, resident in France, made a will in French form disposing of land on trust for sale, which had not yet been sold, the will was held valid under Section 1: *Re Lyne's Trusts*.[1]

In summary, then, Sections 1 and 2 make provisions for wills of citizens of the United Kingdom and Colonies of personal estate, which supplement and overlap the basic rules that for immovables the *lex situs*, and for movables the testator's domiciliary law as at death, regulate the formal validity of wills.

(iii) Essential Validity

The validity of the actual dispositions of a will of movables is determined by the *lex domicilii* of the testator at death; of immovables by the *lex situs* of the land in question. In each case, the law is, of course, that which would be applied had the case come before the courts of the domiciliary state or of the *situs*, as the case may be; in other words, if relevant, the *renvoi* operates.

Thus the type of disposition which may be made is regulated by the *lex domicilii* or, for immovables, the *lex situs*. In *Nelson v. Bridport*,[2] for example, an attempt by Lord Nelson to create by will an entail in Sicilian land failed because such interests were unknown in Sicilian law. Similarly, no effect would be given, in an English court, to a purported life interest in movable property, if the *lex domicilii* of the testator recognized only absolute ownership.

A question of particular importance in the present connection is the restriction of the power of testation common in many systems derived from the Roman law. The English municipal rule has long been complete freedom to dispose of one's property as one would; one of the possibly less desirable manifestations of the spirit of liberty which characterizes the common law. For it could enable a man, say, to leave his all to a mistress, ignoring the moral duty which he owed to his wife and family. Some amelioration of this injustice is now provided by the Inheritance (Family Provisions) Act 1938,[3] which enables dependants to apply to the court for reasonable maintenance to be provided

[1] [1919] 1 Ch. 80
[2] (1846) 8 Beav. 547
[3] As now amended by the Intestates' Estates Act 1952.

for them out of the estate of a person who died domiciled in England; but the principle of free testation as such is unaffected. On these matters, the law governing the succession—the *lex situs* or the *lex domicilii* at death—is decisive. In *Re Groos*,[1] a woman, when domiciled in Holland, made a will leaving all her movable property to her husband, save for 'the legitimate portion to which my descendants are entitled'; she died domiciled in England. In Dutch law, her children would have been entitled to three-quarters of her estate; it was in fact held that the husband could take the whole of his wife's estate. Under the law of her domicile at death, English law, her descendants had no legitimate portion. Conversely, in *Re Annesley*,[2] where a British subject died domiciled in France, her will was held subject to French law and thus her power of testation limited in the interests of her issue.

(iv) Construction

The construction of a will of movables is certainly governed by the law intended by the testator. Thus, if a man leaves property to his 'next-of-kin', the persons comprised in that description would be ascertained by reference to the law chosen by the testator to govern the interpretation of his will. If an express choice is made in the will, e.g., 'I desire these dispositions to be read in accordance with the provisions of English law', clearly no difficulties arise. But in fact it is very rarely that such explicit selection is made and then the court has to determine the testator's implied choice. In this connection, again, the basic presumption is in favour of the testator's domiciliary law at death. Thus, in *Re Fergusson's Will*,[3] a domiciled Englishman bequeathed property to the 'next-of-kin' of a German: those entitled as such under German law were different from those who would be eligible under English law: it was held that English law determined the class of beneficiaries. It must, however, be borne in mind that this is only a presumption—or rather an inference—which might well be displaced upon a consideration of the general circumstances of the will, e.g., its form, the use of the technical terms of a legal system other than that of the domicile,

[1] [1915] 1 Ch. 572
[2] [1926] 1 Ch. 692
[3] [1902] 1 Ch. 483

etc. In *Re Manners*,[1] a domiciled Englishman had died in Nicaragua leaving a will in Spanish and the court held that Spanish law governed its interpretation. Again, in *Re Price*,[2] where a domiciled Frenchwoman had left a will in French form, saying that she wished it to be 'considered the same in England as in France', English law was preferred to that of her French domicile in construing the document. No categorical statement is possible, for the testator's intention, as evinced in all the circumstances of each case, is decisive.

Just as the *lex domicilii* yields place in interpreting wills of movables, so the place of the *lex situs* in the construction of wills of immovables is a matter of some complexity. It may be, for instance, that X makes one will purporting to dispose of land in both Italy and England to his 'heir'; surely it cannot be supposed that he intended that term to be interpreted differently in respect of each piece of land. Accordingly, English law has adopted for immovables, no less than for movables, the basic principle that the law intended by the testator governs the construction of wills, with a presumption—in the absence of evidence to the contrary—in favour of the domiciliary law of the testator at death. Thus, in *Studd v. Cook*,[3] a domiciled Englishman, owning land in both Scotland and England, left a will couched in English terms, purporting to dispose of all his property to X for life with remainder to his sons in entail: the House of Lords held that English law governed the construction of the whole will.

At the same time, the *lex situs* is of great importance in the matter; for if, as is very probable, the testator disposing of land uses technical expressions appropriate to the law of the place where his land is situate, that might well constitute evidence of his intention to select the *lex situs* to govern the interpretation of his will. A devise of Blackacre in Kent to 'A for life without impeachment of waste, remainder to the first and other sons of B in tail male' in the will of a Frenchman domiciled in Belgium would surely indicate that English law was to govern the construction of the document.

Moreover, if the disposition be one which, on proper con-

[1] [1923] 1 Ch. 220
[2] [1900] 1 Ch. 442
[3] (1883) 8 App. Cas. 577

struction under the law intended by the testator, would not be permitted by the *lex situs*, then it would be ineffective. Thus, in *Nelson v. Bridport*, though there could be no doubt that Nelson's will, interpreted according to English law, intended to create an entail in Sicilian land, that purpose failed by reason of Sicilian law. In short, the *lex situs* must of necessity always have the last word, by reason of its effective control of the property. Perhaps the best proposition which may be advanced is this: the construction of a will of immovables is governed by the law intended by the testator which, in the absence of other intent, will be presumed to be the *lex domicilii* of the testator at death; if, however, the disposition so determined conflicts with the provisions of the *lex situs*, the latter prevails.

Section 3 of Lord Kingsdown's Act, which will be more fully discussed in connection with revocation of wills, provides that, 'No will or other testamentary instrument shall be held to be revoked or to have become invalid, nor shall the construction thereof be altered by reason of any change of domicile of the person making the same.' So far as this relates to construction, it is thought that it adds nothing to the common law rule. In the absence of any indication of intention by the testator, construction is governed by his domiciliary law as at death. Section 3 merely indicates that, if his will intrinsically reveals any selection of a law to govern the construction, the fact that he has changed his domicile between making the will and his death will not affect that selection.

(*v*) *Capacity of Beneficiaries*

Even if the will be valid in all other respects, the intended beneficiaries must be capable of taking under it. In English private international law, a legatee or heir may take movables devised to him, if he has capacity to do so by either the law of the testator's domicile at death or his own domiciliary law. In *Re Hellman's Will*,[1] a domiciled Englishman had left legacies to each of the children of a domiciled German, a girl aged eighteen and a boy of seventeen. By the law of Hamburg at the time, a girl attained capacity at eighteen, males at twenty-two. It was held that the girl might receive her legacy at once, being competent under her

[1] (1866) L.R. 2 Eq. 363

lex domicilii to give a receipt therefor, and that the boy might receive his on attaining twenty-one, when by English law, the law of the testator's domicile, he would be of full age. Principle suggests that, in the case of immovables, the question would be determined by the *lex situs* of the property concerned.

(*vi*) *Revocation*

As a will does not operate until the death of its maker, it may be revoked before that event and will consequently never effectively determine the disposition of the testator's property after his death. That, of course, is subject to the proviso that the relevant law—the *lex domicilii* for movables, the *lex situs* for immovables—permits revocation in the circumstances.[1]

Whether a will has been revoked will largely depend on the circumstances of the alleged revocation. If a person makes a later will of movables, valid according to the rules for such wills, in which he purports to revoke the previous will, that revocation will be valid, the new document being the testator's last testament: *Cottrell v. Cottrell.*[2] And, though there is no direct authority, there can be no doubt of the validity of a similar proposition in respect of immovables.

In the case of other alleged revocations, it is thought that, subject to one qualification, the question whether a will has been revoked depends, in the case of movables, upon the law of the testator's domicile at the time of the event claimed to have revoked the will; for immovables, upon the *lex situs*. Suppose that X, domiciled in Arcadia, disclaims but does not destroy a will which he has made and later dies domiciled in England. In English law, in general, it is not sufficient merely to disclaim a will in order to revoke it—it must be destroyed: by Arcadian law, renunciation is an effective revocation. So far as movable property is concerned, X should, on the view here taken, be held to have died intestate. Although by the law of his domicile at death the document would be a valid will, it had been deprived of all validity by an act which, under his then domiciliary law, would have that effect. Subsequent events like a change of domicile should not operate to revive that which was extinct. As to

[1] cf. the doctrine of mutual wills in English law.
[2] (1872) L.R. 2 P. & D. 397

immovables, the *lex situs* would be decisive: if his act in Arcadia would, under that law, deprive X's will of effect, then again he would die intestate.

The qualification referred to arises out of the rule known in some legal systems, including English law, that a will made before marriage is automatically revoked by the testator's marriage.[1] Such a provision is regarded by English courts as a rule not of the law of succession, but of marriage law. Consequently, in private international law, the effect of his marriage upon a testator's will is determined by the law governing the marriage, i.e., the law of the intended matrimonial domicile, usually the husband's domicile at the time of marriage.[2] In *Re Martin*,[3] two French people married in England, the woman having earlier made a will of movables in England, but were domiciled in France at the time that the woman died. The Court of Appeal, finding that at the time of marriage both were domiciled in England, held that the will was revoked under English law and so the woman died intestate. In the case of immovables, again, it would be for the *lex situs* to determine the effect, if any, of the testator's marriage on his will.

Such, it is thought, is the general position. Some obscurity, however, is caused by Section 3 of Lord Kingsdown's Act, which must be again cited: 'No will or other testamentary instrument shall be held to be revoked or to have become invalid, nor shall the construction thereof be altered by reason of any change of domicile of the person making the same.' It will be noted that there is no specific concern—as was the case in Sections 1 and 2—with the formal validity of wills of personalty of British subjects; and this change of wording has led to the suggestion that Section 3 is of general application, affecting the wills of aliens no less than of British subjects, all forms of property and not merely personalty, and regulating essential validity no less than form.

It must be conceded also that such a suggestion derives support from the case, *In Bonis Groos*.[4] A Dutchwoman married a

[1] Unless made in contemplation of that marriage.
[2] *De Reneville v. De Reneville* [1948] P. 100
[3] [1900] P. 211
[4] [1904] P. 269

Dutchman in Holland, having previously made a will there in Dutch form; both parties were at all material times domiciled in Holland. Subsequently, they became domiciled in England where the woman now died. The question was whether the will was revoked by reason of her marriage, an effect which would have ensued under English law. The judge held that it was not revoked, adducing among other reasons the words of Section 3, 'No will . . . shall be held to be revoked . . . by reason of any change of domicile . . .'

It may, however, be observed that the English rule of revocation by marriage is a matter of matrimonial law, not of succession, and would operate accordingly only if England was, at marriage, the intended matrimonial home: *Re Martin*. That was not the case in *In Bonis Groos*. In any case, if the rule had been relevant, the revocation would have been the result not of the change of domicile merely, but of the marriage of the testatrix. Section 3 was thus quite inapplicable. The judge indeed fully recognized that he could base his decision on the simple ground that revocation by marriage is a question of matrimonial law and was not a part of the Dutch law which governed the marriage of the deceased. *In Bonis Groos* should be regarded as based upon that ground.

A fundamental objection to the suggestion mentioned as to the scope of Section 3, is that it would nullify completely the common law rule that the *lex domicilii* of the testator at death governs the substance of his will. For, if a will, which would be valid if the testator had died as soon as he had made it, is not to be revoked by a change of domicile, then it would obviously be unnecessary to satisfy the law of the testator's ultimate domicile. But the authorities clearly show that the law of the last domicile in the case of movables, and the *lex situs* for immovables, govern the devolution of the testator's property.

It still remains however to determine what is the ambit of Section 3. In this connection, it is pertinent to recall that the Act is designated one to deal with the will of personal estate of British subjects. It may accordingly be submitted that Section 3, no less than Sections 1 and 2, is concerned with such wills. This would mean that the intention of Section 3 was that, if a British subject made a will of personalty which would be formally valid if the testator had died immediately after making it, it should not be invalidated merely by reason of a change of his domicile, so far as English courts are concerned. As an example, suppose that a British subject domiciled in Scotland made a will in Scottish form while on holiday in England and later died domiciled in Spain where special formalities, not observed in this case, were necessary. It will be seen that the will is not formally preserved under either Section 1 or Section 2: but had he died immediately after making the will, it would have been valid under the common law rule and it is thought that Section 3 now preserves it. This means of course that it is preserved *as to form* by Section 3; the law of Spain would be decisive as to the effect of the will. It is true that such an interpretation of Section 3 would indicate a special preference for British subjects, for it is obvious that the will of, say, a Frenchman dying domiciled in Spain would not be similarly preserved. But the title of the Act, anyhow, would suggest that special treatment for British subjects was in fact the statute's purpose.

In short, it is suggested that the section is to be read as if it said, 'No will or other testamentary instrument of a British subject as to personal estate shall be held to be revoked or to have become invalid formally, nor shall the construction thereof be altered by reason of any change of domicile of the person making the same.'[1] To use again the example of the British subject dying domiciled in Spain with a will of personalty made in Scots form; the testator's change of domicile to Spain would not invalidate the will as to form nor would it alter its construction: the use of Scots technical terms, say, would suggest that Scots law governed the construction, even though the testator died domiciled in Spain. But the validity of the dispositions would be governed by Spanish law in so far as they concerned movables, by the *lex situs* for any immovables disposed of. If this suggestion be correct, it will be seen that Section 3 is in fact of very limited effect.

[1] Cf. Practice Direction [1953] 1 W.L.R. 1237, at p. 1240:
Lord Kingsdown's Act—This Act can be used only for curing faults of execution, and appointing executors, but no further. It cannot make good, for example, the will of a minor the law of whose domicile does not permit him to make a will.

CHAPTER SIX

RECOGNITION AND ENFORCEMENT OF FOREIGN JUDGMENTS

THIS chapter concerns the circumstances in which an English court will recognize and give effect to judgments delivered in the courts of another state.[1] That the tribunals of civilized states should acknowledge the validity of one another's adjudications needs no justification, if it be granted that all are imbued with the same spirit of impartial inquiry into the disputes which come before them, and the same desire to administer justice. If all judgments were recognized everywhere, an ideal regularity would prevail throughout the world; varying attitudes on questions of public policy and differences of classification of disputes, however, make such a prospect utopian.

In most modern systems of law, the basis of recognition of judgments delivered in another jurisdiction is reciprocity. English law also adopts that principle in its modern statutory provisions for the enforcement of foreign judgments, as will be seen hereafter. The common law attitude of English private international law is, however, broader based. Provided that it complies with certain requirements, a foreign judgment will be respected and, if necessary, given effect in this country, without a jealous search for satisfaction that the courts of the country concerned would accord similar treatment to an English award.

At common law, this is not done by direct enforcement of the foreign order in England. In the case of an English judgment, the court has the means of ensuring compliance with its order—the various writs of execution which authorize the sheriff to seize the property of the judgment debtor and cause its sale to provide funds to satisfy the judgment creditor; bankruptcy of the judgment debtor; in some circumstances, indeed, his imprisonment. To allow such direct enforcement in England of, say, an Italian judgment would be, in effect, to treat the order of the Italian court—which is, of course, the representative of the sovereign

[1] Other than those in matters of personal status, for which see Chap. Two.

authority of Italy—as effective in itself to control the conduct and regulate the property rights of persons in England. The cherished principle of state sovereignty within state territory prevents such liberality, at least not without the authority of the legislature.

The common law method of giving effect to foreign judgments is to allow the party successful in the foreign proceedings to bring an action in England on the judgment. The principle underlying this action is that the foreign judgment imposes an obligation on the defendant vis-à-vis the plaintiff to observe such order as may have been made against him. This, it is thought, represents an admirable middle course between direct enforcement of any foreign orders and the adoption of the rather niggardly 'tit-for-tat' principle of reciprocity. Just as parties may impose upon themselves by agreement enforceable obligations of any content, so long as the agreement bears the characteristics which mark it legally as a contract; so, whatever the cause of action and basis of adjudication, a foreign award which bears the characteristics which, in English eyes, make it a judgment, imposes an obligation for which an English court will secure respect. Indeed, Lord Esher M.R. once stated that 'the liability of the defendant arises upon an implied contract to pay the amount of the foreign judgment'.

The treatment of the foreign order as a source of obligation and not, strictly, as an enforceable order in itself, explains a difference in effect between English and foreign judgments. In English law itself, the rule is that a judgment of the court consumes the original cause of action. If A sues B for damages for, say, breach of contract, then, once the judgment has been delivered, A cannot sue B in respect of the same claim again. In place of the former liability of B to do for A whatever the contract required him to do, there is now a higher, more august, liability upon B, namely to pay A the sum of damages that the court has awarded. At common law, however, a foreign judgment does not, in the eyes of an English court, consume the original cause of action. Suppose that A sues B in respect of a contract in Italy and is given judgment; he could thereafter either bring an action against B to enforce the Italian judgment as such, or could instead sue B again in England on the original contractual claim, using the Italian judgment as evidence of his right's existence.

The choice is A's. In other words, the foreign judgment merely adds an alternative obligation to the existing cause of action.[1]

Again, in English law, the principle known as '*res judicata*' (a decided issue) in general ensures that a judgment, once given, is conclusive of the facts with which it deals as between the same parties (and against all the world in the case of a judgment *in rem*) in the event of another dispute involving the same subject-matter. If A brings an action in England against B, claiming that B owes him £500 under a contract and the action fails, then a subsequent attempt by A to sue B on the same ground would be met by the defence of *res judicata*—that issue has been decided: there is no debt of £500 due from B to A. This principle applies only partially to foreign judgments: an unsuccessful claim in a foreign court is a bar to an action by the same plaintiff on the same cause of action in England: *Ricardo v. Garcias.*[2] The last paragraph shows that it does not apply in the case of successful foreign actions.

Though the common law is liberal in its attitude towards the recognition of foreign judgments, it can be seen that its position is not very logical. Judgment against the foreign plaintiff in his foreign action prevents his further suing the defendant in England on the same cause of action; but a foreign order in his favour does not prevent his doing so, if that be his wish. Moreover, the judgment itself, if he seek to enforce it here, is regarded as imposing on the defendant an obligation alternative to, not extinctive of, that which was the cause of action in the foreign court. Needless to say, of course, satisfaction of either prevents action on the other—the plaintiff could not get his damages under the foreign award and sue again in England.

As already indicated, there has, since 1868, been a series of enactments providing for the more or less direct enforcement in England of foreign judgments in certain circumstances. These statutes, however, are not all-embracing. The number of foreign states to which their provisions are applicable is very limited, with the result that the common law enforcement of foreign orders is still of primary importance. The common law rules are, in

[1] Contrast the provisions of the Foreign Judgments (Reciprocal Enforcement) Act 1933 post.

[2] (1845) 12 Cl. & F. 368

consequence, first considered and then the provisions of the various statutes.

A. Common Law Enforcement

The general characteristics of common law enforcement of foreign judgments have been already indicated; here it is necessary to consider what judgments will be so enforceable. The English rule is that an action may be brought upon the judgment of a foreign court, provided that

(i) the court was one of competent jurisdiction and
(ii) the order was final and conclusive.

Each requirement may be separately considered.

(*i*) *Jurisdiction*

The principal requirement is that the foreign court should have been competent to entertain the action, a matter which the English court, now asked to recognize the judgment, determines for itself. English private international law is, for these purposes, the touchstone of foreign jurisdiction. In many continental states, the presence of property of the defendant within the jurisdiction empowers the court to hear suits against him; e.g., suppose that X in Germany has a claim arising out of business dealings against Y, whose base is in England but who has stock stored in a warehouse in Hamburg; a German court would be, in German law, entitled to hear X's claim and make an order against Y, regardless of Y's participation in the proceedings or not. A judgment so obtained in Germany, however, would not be regarded by an English court as the decision of a court of competent jurisdiction, if Y did not participate.[1]

So far as jurisdiction *in personam* is concerned, the principal tests for foreign, as for English courts, are effectiveness and submission. A foreign court will be considered to have effective jurisdiction if the defendant to the action was present in the state in which the court sits, at the time that proceedings were commenced. In *Carrick v. Hancock*,[2] for instance, a person domiciled in England was served with notice of proceedings against him in the Swedish court, while he was on a short visit to Sweden.

[1] cf. *Emanuel v. Symon* [1908] 1 K.B. 302
[2] (1895) 12 T.L.R. 59

He returned very soon after to England and took no further part in the Swedish action, in which judgment was eventually given against him. The fact of his presence in Sweden at the commencement of the action was held to ground the jurisdiction of the Swedish court and the judgment was enforceable against him in England. In the case of corporations, the existence of a definite place within the jurisdiction from which the corporation is doing business would suffice to constitute presence of the corporation in that state.

In like manner, if the parties choose to submit their disputes to the courts of a state other than that which would normally have jurisdiction over them, the fact of their submission is, generally speaking, enough to vest the court concerned with authority to determine any claim. Thus, in *Feyericke v. Hubbard*,[1] a British subject domiciled and resident in England had agreed in a contract with a Belgian company that 'all disputes as to the present agreement and its fulfilment shall be submitted to Belgian jurisdiction': it was held that a judgment of the Belgian court obtained by the company, in default of appearance by the Englishman, was enforceable in England as the order of a competent court.

Express submission of this type raises no problems; but jurisdiction may be impliedly conferred, by the conduct of the parties, upon a foreign court. To commence an action in the courts of a given state would obviously confer jurisdiction upon them, so far as the plaintiff is concerned: if A chooses to commence proceedings in the court of Ruritania, he cannot subsequently be allowed to say that that court was incompetent to entertain his claim. Again, if B were to put in a defence in an action so commenced whereby he pleaded to the merits of the dispute, he would be deemed to have conceded the competence of the court to hear the action. Suppose that the claim was for breach of contract and B's defence was limited to denying the contract or saying that he had not been guilty of a breach of contract, he would be taken to concede the jurisdiction of the Ruritanian court to deal with the claim.

The case would be different if, though making an appearance in the proceedings, B did so only to demur to the competence of

[1] (1902) 71 L.J.K.B. 509

the court to hear the claim. It seems obvious common sense that, if a person appeared before a court only to deny that the court was entitled to hear the claim against him, such person could not be said to submit to the court. On this self-evident proposition, some doubt was formerly cast by the case of *Harris v. Taylor.*[1] There, the defendant, who was at all times domiciled and resident in England, was made party to an action in the Isle of Man, the plaintiff having obtained leave of the Manx court to serve him out of the Manx jurisdiction on the ground that the cause of action, a tort, had arisen within the Isle of Man. The defendant applied to have the proceedings stayed for a variety of reasons—that the Manx rules of procedure did not allow such service and that there was no cause of action within the Manx jurisdiction among them. On the rejection of this protest, the defendant took no further part in the proceedings, in which judgment was given against him. The Manx plaintiff now sought to enforce this judgment in England and the Court of Appeal held him entitled to do so. The Court appears to have been of opinion that the defendant, by entering a protest instead of merely remaining absolutely quiet and ignoring the Manx action, must be taken to have acknowledged the jurisdiction of the court.

One answer to this might have been that, by raising the question whether a tort had been committed within the Isle of Man, the defendant did in fact plead to the merits of the case as well as querying the jurisdiction of the court. In *Re Dulles' Settlement Trusts,*[2] however, the Court of Appeal itself has recently provided an authoritative explanation of *Harris v. Taylor*. In this case, the Court held that a father did not submit to English jurisdiction when he entered appearance to an action in England in order to contest the competence of the court to make an order against him for the maintenance of his child. Of the earlier decision, the Court said that the defendant had been served in England under a Manx provision which authorized such service in respect of a tort committed within the jurisdiction. His denial of such tort having been rejected by the court, he must be taken to have been correctly served, by Manx rules, under the principle mentioned. And since that rule was identical with a rule

[1] [1915] 2 K.B. 580
[2] [1951] Ch. 265

by which English courts themselves, under Order XI,[1] assume jurisdiction, it followed that the English court would be obliged to recognize the validity of the Manx jurisdiction, regardless of any question of voluntary submission by the defendant to the Manx Court. In other words, *Harris v. Taylor* is an authority not on submission but on the reciprocal recognition of statutory jurisdiction; and is no obstacle to adoption of the simple principle that denial of the jurisdiction of the court concerned does not constitute acceptance of its competence.

This explanation of *Harris v. Taylor*, taken with the matrimonial cases of *Boettcher v. Boettcher*[2] and *Travers v. Holley*,[3] points to an important recent common law development—namely that English courts will also recognize the competence of a court which took jurisdiction on a statutory basis in circumstances in which, *mutatis mutandis*, English courts themselves would have been empowered to determine the dispute between the parties, regardless of the fact that the defendant neither was present nor submitted to the jurisdiction of the court. In *Boettcher v. Boettcher*, the validity was upheld of an American divorce, granted in the absence of one of the parties, because the rules of procedure of the American state concerned were substantially similar to those in England, whereby actual notice of proceedings on the defendant, in some circumstances, may be dispensed with. This is of great importance in view of the modern tendency of states to extend their jurisdiction by municipal legislation, a trend of which the English Order XI is a fair example. In such circumstances, it is usually not easy to suggest that the jurisdiction is based upon either effectiveness or submission; it is consequently a laudable achievement of the common law of England to evolve a rule that directs recognition of statutory jurisdiction in circumstances where English courts themselves would have a similar competence.

It has frequently been suggested that the nationality of the parties is a ground of jurisdiction, e.g., that a French court would always be competent to hear an action, the parties to which were French nationals. Evershed M.R., indeed, has said, '. . . there is no

[1] R.S.C. Order XI r. 1 (ee); cf. Chapter One, ante p. 38
[2] [1949] W.N. 83
[3] Chapter Two, ante, p. 59

doubt that it is competent for the courts of a particular country, in a suit between persons who are either nationals or subjects of that country or are otherwise subject to their jurisdiction, to make orders in personam against such a party'.[1] It is stressed, however, that in no case has the nationality of the parties or either of them been the necessary ground of the jurisdiction of the court concerned: and *dicta*, however eminent their author, are not authoritative. It would surely be preposterous that a Jamaican could be made defendant to an action in an English court on no other ground than that he happens to be a citizen of the United Kingdom and Colonies: the possibilities become even more alarming when one reflects upon the number of persons of dual nationality in the world, e.g., the Frenchman who is also a United Kingdom citizen because he was born in England. It is therefore strongly urged that nationality is, in law, no basis of jurisdiction and that the only grounds recognized at common law, in personal actions, are effectiveness, submission, and the substantial identity of the basis of the foreign court's assumption of competence with that which an English court could exercise.

A judgment *in rem* by a foreign court will be recognized in England only if the foreign court concerned had effective jurisdiction, i.e., if the subject matter of the dispute was situate in the foreign state at the time of the action.[2]

(ii) Final and Conclusive Judgment

In addition to the need that the court be competent, there is the further requirement that the judgment delivered be 'final and conclusive'. Somewhat misleadingly, perhaps, this does not require that there can be no appeal from the judgment: to use an English example, a decision of the High Court could be final and conclusive in the present sense, although appeal to the Court of Appeal is possible. What is meant is that the judgment must be unalterable by the court which delivered it and that no further order of that court would be necessary before it would be enforceable in the state where it was given. This is one reason why awards of alimony or maintenance in foreign divorce proceedings, orders for child maintenance, etc., are generally unenforceable—

[1] *British Nylon Spinners v. I.C.I.* [1952] 2 All E.R. 780, 782
[2] *Castrique v. Imrie* (1870) L.R. 4 H.L. 414

save as to arrears, which have accrued due as a definite debt. Such orders are invariably liable to review and alteration by the court which makes them, if there be any change in the circumstances of the parties concerned.

The leading authoritative instances of the present requirement are *Nouvion v. Freeman*[1] and *Harrop v. Harrop*.[2] In the former, N had obtained a so-called 'remate' judgment against H in Spain in respect of a sale of property in that country and now sought to enforce this Spanish judgment in England against H's estate. It appeared that, in the Spanish procedure for the recovery of debts, a remate judgment was obtainable upon the plaintiff's establishing a *prima facie* case: this did not, however, prevent either party from going on to institute full proceedings for trial of the issue between them; and, moreover, if the defendant to the remate proceedings chose to take the latter course, he could not be met with the defence of *res judicata* based on the remate judgment given in his opponent's favour. The House of Lords held that the remate judgment could not be considered final and conclusive and thus that it could not be enforced here.

In *Harrop v. Harrop*, a woman sought to enforce against her husband a maintenance order given in her favour in Perak. Under the law operative in Perak, application had to be made to the magistrate in order to enforce a maintenance order and, on the application, the magistrate could vary the order if he saw fit. The woman's action failed. 'In my view,' said Sankey J., 'a judgment or order cannot be said to be final and conclusive if an order has to be obtained for its enforcement and on the application for such an order the original judgment is liable to be abrogated or varied.'

A final requirement, applicable in the case of a judgment *in personam*, is that the order which it is sought to enforce here must be for a sum certain of money.

As stated at the outset, a judgment final in the above sense and delivered by a competent court will be recognized and enforceable in England, without inquiry into its substance. The fact that the adjudicating court reached an erroneous decision will not invalidate that decision, any more than would the

[1] (1889) 15 App. Cas. 1
[2] [1920] 3 K.B. 386

unwisdom of the obligation assumed by a person under a contract prevent its enforcement against him—subject, of course, to the scrutiny of public policy and the absence of fraud. To use the common expression, there can be no impeachment of a foreign judgment on its merits. In *Godard v. Gray*,[1] for example, an action had been brought in the French courts by French plaintiffs against English defendants in a dispute over a contract whose proper law was English. The French court had misconstrued a clause in the contract and assessed the damages awarded to the plaintiffs on the basis of this misinterpretation. The plaintiffs sought to enforce the French judgment in England and succeeded, the English court rejecting the defendant's plea based upon the mistake of the French tribunal.

The reasons for this rule are sound. In the first place, if it were open to attack a foreign judgment on its merits, the result would be that such a judgment would virtually be deprived of effect, since the defendant to an action for enforcement in England would invariably be likely to go into the merits of the case again. If it were a mistake in the application of its own law with which the foreign court was charged,[2] it would not be for an English court to assume the role of a court of appeal from the adjudicating court: it would be gross impertinence for English courts impliedly to assert greater competence in the administration of, say, Italian law than that of an Italian court. Again, a finding of fact by the foreign court, albeit mistaken, would nevertheless be a finding by the tribunal exclusively competent to determine issues of fact, and should no more be reversed here than could the verdict of an English jury.[3] Even a misinterpretation of English law in a foreign court would be a question of fact for that tribunal, just as is proof of foreign law in English courts; and so would have to be treated as a matter of fact, if challenged in an English action to enforce the foreign award. From every point of view, therefore, the inviolability of the foreign judgment on its merits is correct on principle.

[1] (1870) L.R. 6 Q.B. 139

[2] cf. *Pemberton v. Hughes* [1899] 1 Ch. 781

[3] The English method of virtually reversing a jury's verdict on the ground that, in law, there was no evidence to support it, is not applicable in the circumstances here under discussion.

(iii) Defences

The inability to attack a foreign judgment on its merits does not mean that a defendant to an English action brought to enforce the award is limited, in his resistance, to a denial of the jurisdiction of the adjudicating court or of the finality of the decision. In the first place, in this no less than in other fields of private international law, the effects of public policy requirements are felt. No action will be allowed in England to enforce here a judgment which conflicts with English public policy. In a way, this is a breach of the principle just discussed that a foreign judgment cannot be attacked on its merits, for what is really repugnant to English standards is the cause of action on which the judgment is founded.

At the same time, it is sound common sense that this should be so, if public policy is to be conceded a place in the field of private international law. The heads of policy have been noted in Chapter One: to take one example, it would be absurd if English courts would not allow an action to be brought here on a 'blackmailing' contract[1] but would allow the enforcement here of a French judgment which gave damages for breach of such a contract. Hence even the general inviolability of a foreign judgment must yield to the dictates of English public policy.

Again, although not concerned with the *merits* of a foreign judgment other than in relation to public policy, English courts may yet refuse to enforce it because of defects in the method by which the decision of the foreign court was reached; defects which constitute a denial of justice to the party against whom the judgment was given. This defence of 'denial of natural justice', as it is styled, is, in every way, unsatisfactory. In the first place, it involves stigmatizing a foreign tribunal as lacking in the elements of justice, a consideration which probably accounts for the infrequency of its invocation. Then its scope is extremely vague. By reason of the inviolability of judgments on their merits, the fact that the foreign decision is wrong, even blatantly wrong, does not of itself permit the raising of the defence; though the person against whom it was given might not unreasonably feel that he has received an unjust decision. 'The most that can be said with certainty is that any impropriety in the foreign

[1] cf. *Kaufman v. Gerson* [1904] 1 K.B. 591

proceedings which has deprived a party of an opportunity to present his side of the case will be regarded as a violation of natural justice.'[1]

The actual decisions all concern hearings by foreign courts without either due notice to the defendant of the proceedings or, if he was given notice, without his having adequate facilities for the presentation of his case. The first type of case, anyhow, presupposes that he was not present at the commencement of the proceedings and thus that the court acted without jurisdiction.[2] The opportunity to allege denial of natural justice in these circumstances is further limited by reason of English recognition of some forms of substituted service, which correspond to English extensions of jurisdiction. The English court did refuse to recognize an American divorce decree in *Rudd v. Rudd*,[3] where a husband, purporting to divorce his wife who was in England, had initiated proceedings in Washington and inserted a notice in a local newspaper and sent a copy of his petition to an address in England at which the wife had never lived; in consequence, she knew nothing of the action until she eventually heard that she had been divorced. In *Boettcher v. Boettcher*, on the other hand, an Indiana decree dissolving the marriage of a woman resident in England was recognized, although the woman had in fact been unaware of the proceedings, because the Indiana procedure, which the petitioning husband had properly employed, was essentially similar to that possible in England. A procedure which we use ourselves could scarcely be stigmatized as contrary to natural justice.

Moreover, certainly in a matter of personal status, a decision of the courts of the domiciliary state will be recognized, whatever he circumstances. Since the domiciliary law is the governing law in these matters, an English court could scarce deny, say, the divorce of two persons because the circumstances of the granting of the decree in the court of the domicile were repugnant to English notions of fair play. *Boettcher v. Boettcher* might have proceeded on that ground. More strikingly, perhaps, in *Igra v. Igra*, a decree granted in Germany under the Nazi discriminatory

[1] Cheshire, *Private International Law* (4th ed.) p. 632
[2] cf. *Igra v. Igra* [1951] P. 404, per Pearce J.
[3] [1924] P. 72

provisions, dissolving the marriage of a German Jew who was at the time out of Germany as a refugee, was recognized in this country.

The requirement that a party should have a fair opportunity to give his version of the dispute will be satisfied so long as it is open for him to put his case before the court and to meet the allegations of the other side. In *Jacobson v. Frachon*,[1] for instance, the English plaintiffs in an action in France claimed that the French defendant had, in breach of contract, delivered inferior goods. The French court appointed an expert to come to England and examine the goods: the person appointed was in fact related to the defendant and submitted a report which was grossly prejudiced in favour of the defendant, but upon which the court acted, giving judgment against the plaintiffs. The English party now sought to reopen the dispute in England and, when the defendant pleaded the French judgment in his favour, they claimed that it should be rejected as contrary to natural justice. The claim failed. It appeared that the French court had not been bound to accept the expert's report and that the plaintiffs could have challenged the report in the French action, bringing witnesses to France to support their contentions, etc. (Indeed, they had unsuccessfully attacked the report.) In view of the facilities open to them under the French procedure, they could not be said to have suffered a denial of elementary fair play, despite the bias of the report in favour of their opponent; they were thus met, in the English action, with a successful defence of *res judicata*.

Just as the English court might demur to the method by which the foreign court came to its decision as lacking in a sense of elementary justice, so it will refuse to recognize a judgment delivered in an action where the parties or one of them has deceived the court into making that decision, e.g., by giving or procuring false evidence. In short, English courts refuse to acknowledge a judgment which is the result of a fraud practised upon the adjudicating court; and rightly so, for, if that court was misled, the judgment now set up does not really represent the view of the court upon the real dispute which was before it.

Clearly, if fraud be alleged, it will be necessary for the English

[1] (1928) 138 L.T. 386

court to investigate the allegation and ascertain the facts on which it is based. This may necessitate a reopening of the whole case, rehearing of the evidence which was adduced before the foreign court, etc. Consequently, the defence of fraud has been attacked as an infringement of the inviolability of a foreign judgment on its merits. In truth, this is not so. The issue before the English court is not the same as that dealt with by the foreign court whose judgment is impugned. The English court is concerned not to ascertain the rights of the parties in respect of their foreign cause of action but to determine whether the foreign tribunal was misled into the view which it took of those rights. The foreign court itself could hardly have been aware that it was being deceived, and so it is inevitable that the English court should, if necessary, go into matters which were raised and decided in the court concerned.

The defence is thus perfectly justifiable and is well established, the classic illustration being *Abouloff v. Oppenheimer*.[1] In that case, A had recovered judgment against B in an action in a Russian court, in which he claimed that B had unlawfully detained goods belonging to A. B by his defence had alleged that the goods were in A's own possession all the time but his plea was unsuccessful. When A sought to enforce the Russian judgment in England, B pleaded fraud, claiming that A had misled the Russian court by falsely swearing that B had the goods when they were in fact in his own hands. To this defence, A entered a demurrer, i.e., an objection in law, which signified his admission that the facts as stated by B were true. In effect, A conceded that he did perjure himself before the Russian court. Accordingly, the Court of Appeal held B's defence good and dismissed A's action.

Indeed, so important is it that an English court should not give countenance to a fraud and so support, as it were, the hoodwinking of a tribunal of justice in another state, that the defence may be raised in English proceedings on a foreign award, even though the defendant had known the facts at the time of the foreign action but did not raise them in that action. *Syal v. Heyward*[2] in fact arose under the Foreign Judgments (Reciprocal Enforcement) Act 1933 but is of general application in respect of

[1] (1882) 10 Q.B.D. 295
[2] [1948] 2 K.B. 443

fraud. The facts were that S had obtained judgment against H in India on a claim that he had lent them 20,000 rupees and had registered the decision under the 1933 Act. The defendants, H, now sought to have the registration cancelled on the ground that in fact S had advanced only 10,800 rupees, retaining the balance of the 20,000 as interest in fraud of the Indian usury laws, a fact which the form of his claim had concealed from the Indian court. The Court of Appeal held it irrelevant that H could have raised this matter, as they obviously could, in the Indian proceedings. Their defence here raised an issue of fraud which must be ventilated; and, as it was established to the Court's satisfaction that S had indeed acted as alleged, the registration of the Indian judgment was cancelled. It appears therefore that, if the defendant to an English action brought to enforce a foreign judgment can show a *prima facie* case that the foreign court was deceived, the issue will be investigated, whether or not it was, or could have been, raised in the foreign proceedings.

B. Statutory Enforcement of Foreign Judgments

Beside the common law action which has so far been the subject of consideration, there exist three principal statutory provisions relating to the enforcement of decisions of foreign superior courts, extending progressively from the United Kingdom to the Commonwealth and Empire and thence to politically foreign countries also. Some statutory provisions for inferior courts also exist.

The Judgments Extension Act 1868 provides for the mutual enforcement of money judgments between the superior courts of England, Scotland and (since the independence of Eire) Northern Ireland. Under the Act, a judgment of any of these courts, upon registration in another, becomes enforceable *as to execution* in the territory of that other as if it had been initially given in the court of registration. A decision of the Scottish Court of Session, if registered in the Supreme Court in England, will thus be enforceable for execution purposes in England as if it had been given in the first place in the High Court.

It is to be observed however that the scope of the Act is limited. In the first place, only money judgments are so registrable; i.e., judgments for the payment of debts, damages, or costs.

Again, the effect of registration is only to permit execution of the judgment in England; that is to say, the issue of the writs of *fieri facias*, *elegit*, etc., which authorize the taking of the defendant's property for sale in satisfaction of the judgment. Non-satisfaction of a judgment registered in England under the Act would not authorize the service of a bankruptcy notice, a process which is possible in respect of an English judgment. A Scottish or Northern Ireland judgment creditor who wishes to use the registration procedure may do so as of right within twelve months; thereafter, the leave of the court must be obtained. It may be noted finally that the Act does not exclude the adoption, instead, of the common law process of action to enforce a judgment. A Scots plaintiff, for instance, who has been successful in his Scottish action, could either register his judgment in England under the Act or, at his option, bring an action here to enforce it at common law.

Under the Administration of Justice Act 1920, provision was made for registration of judgments as between the superior courts of United Kingdom countries and those of the Dominions and other British territories, including protectorates. The Act applies in respect of such territories only if extended to them by Order in Council and an Order is made only where the territory in question has similar arrangements for judgments of the courts of the home countries. The principle thus is one of reciprocity of arrangement for recognition, not of recognition of judgments as such; in which connection it will be noticed that the reciprocity principle is one for the Administration to act on in deciding whether to make an Order and not for the court to consider in individual cases.

Like the 1868 Act, the 1920 Act applies only to money judgments and again makes them, when registered, enforceable only for the purpose of execution. There are, however, important differences between the provisions of the two Acts. By the 1920 Act, a person who has been awarded judgment in one of the territories may apply for registration of the judgment in the High Court in England or Northern Ireland or in the Scottish Court of Session, which courts may order that it be registered, if they consider it to be convenient and just that it should be enforced in the United Kingdom.

This means that, in contrast with the position under the

1868 Act, the court in England has a discretion whether to register the judgment or not. There are, further, some circumstances in which the court *must* refuse registration. Broadly, these circumstances correspond with the common law requirements for a successful action for enforcement, with the exception and addition that a judgment from which an appeal is pending in the court of adjudication must not be registered.

As under the 1868 Act, the common law procedure remains an alternative process; but the 1920 Act discourages its adoption, by providing that failure to seek registration of a registrable judgment will result in a successful plaintiff's being deprived of his costs in the common law action.

The 1920 Act has been extended to a number of territories, including New Zealand, several Australian states, Saskatchewan, Newfoundland and some colonies. Since 1933, however, it is no longer adopted for new territories by reason of the passing in that year of the more comprehensive Foreign Judgments (Reciprocal Enforcement) Act. This statute again makes provision for registration of judgments on a basis of reciprocity. It is applicable to both British and non-British countries which make similar arrangements for English judgments, though, hitherto, among foreign countries, it has been extended only to France and Belgium, Burma, India and Pakistan.

Again only money judgments are affected but for the rest there is some modification of the principles of the earlier statutes. Judgments of the superior courts of states to which the Act extends are registrable here up to six years from the time of their delivery. Moreover, if the judgment be registrable, it must be registered: the court has not the discretion given under the 1920 Act and the common law action is barred as an alternative to registration. But, though the judgment must be registered upon application, there is a series of circumstances in which the registration *must* be set aside, e.g., if the adjudicating court had no jurisdiction, the judgment was obtained by fraud, etc. It is further provided that the registration may be set aside if the matter which was in dispute in the foreign action had already previously been the subject of an action between the parties in a competent court; in effect, if the defence of *res judicata* would have been available in the foreign action.

The effect of registration under the 1933 Act is wider than in the case of the earlier statutes. After registration, the foreign judgment is, *for all purposes*, as effective as if it had originally been delivered in the High Court; hence it would be possible, e.g., to make an unsatisfied French judgment, which had been registered, the subject of English bankruptcy proceedings.

It may be mentioned in conclusion that neither the 1868 nor the 1920 Act affects the right of a person, successful in a foreign action, to bring an action in England on the same *cause of action*. The 1933 Act, in this connection, is more doubtful. Section 6 provides 'No proceedings for the payment of a sum payable under a foreign judgment, being a judgment to which this Part of this Act applies, other than proceedings by way of registration of the judgment, shall be entertained by any court in the United Kingdom'. The Section would clearly appear to intend that, where a judgment is given in a foreign action which can be registered, then only registration procedure shall be used here. However, a new English action on the original cause of action would not, strictly speaking, be a proceeding 'for the payment of a sum payable under a foreign judgment'. Bearing in mind the general tendency of English courts to interpret statutes in the literal sense of the words they use, it may well be that, though no common law action could be brought to enforce a judgment registrable under the 1933 Act, a suit might be brought again on the claim which was made before the foreign court.

Although little used yet, the 1933 Act is potentially applicable in respect of superior court judgments in any part of the world. In the matter of judgments of inferior courts, however, statutory provision has so far been made only within the United Kingdom, apart from the maintenance order regulations noted in Chapter Two. The Inferior Courts Judgments Extension Act 1882 extends the judgments of inferior courts, such as county courts, throughout the United Kingdom by provisions substantially the same as those of the Judgments Extension Act 1868. Save where that Act is applicable, the common law process would have to be employed.

CHAPTER SEVEN

PROCEDURE AND EVIDENCE

ONE of the earliest rules of private international law to emerge—and one which has steadily retained universal support—is that matters of procedure are governed by the *lex fori*. The necessity of the principle is patent. Private international law cases arise in the same courts of a given state or jurisdiction, which deal with purely domestic issues. The fact that one or both of the parties may be foreign or that some other system of law may be found appropriate to determine what are the rights of the parties cannot require the court to adopt also the rules of procedure of that system. It would be an impossible imposition, e.g., upon English courts to expect French procedure in dealing with a contract whose proper law is French, or German procedure in an action by a German claiming damages for injuries caused by a negligent act done in Germany. English courts may be resorted to by persons whose rights are governed by French or German law; but in asserting those rights, such persons must accept and comply with the procedure of the courts of their choice.

The exclusive control of the *lex fori* over matters of procedure, however, can be of the greatest importance in private international law. Whether a given matter is one of procedure is a problem of classification which itself will be decided by the *lex fori*. Consequently, the wider the view taken by the court of what constitutes a question of procedure, the more prominent will be the application and influence of the internal law of the *forum* in 'foreign element' cases. Suppose, for instance, that Arcadian law regards all matters of limitation of actions as procedural and, in Arcadian law, no action may be brought more than three years after the accrual of the cause of action. If A sues B in Arcadia for payment of a debt due under a contract governed by Ruritanian law four years after the debt first became payable, he will fail; even though, under Ruritanian law, the period may be six years and the debt thus still claimable. The tendency to classify questions as matters of procedure is a marked feature of

English law; a characteristic, natural perhaps in a system where the law has grown from decisions—for decisions depend upon actions, and thinking in terms of actions is inevitably thinking in terms of procedure. This chapter concerns some of the questions of procedure in English law which are important in private international law.

A. Parties

Perhaps the first question which arises in connection with the commencement of an action is, Are all the necessary persons made parties to the action, whether as plaintiffs or as defendants? This is regarded as procedural because it affects the manner in which a right may be enforced. For instance, if A has issued process against B, it may not be disputed that A is entitled to something from B; but it may be that, because his right is shared by C, A can enforce it only if C joins in his action. Hence, in an English suit, English rules relating to the joinder of parties must be observed. By way of example, though an English partnership may be sued in its trade name, that rule does not apply to foreign firms unless they have a place of business in England.[1] Hence, if B and C trade in Ruritania as, say, 'Ruriproducts', an action by A in England against Ruriproducts for breach of a contract made in Ruritania and governed by Ruritanian law would be misconceived; he must claim against B and C as such, and the action would be A v. B and C.[2]

B. Limitation of Actions

Though the action be properly constituted, it may be that the time has passed within which the claim might be prosecuted. It is clearly sound policy that the law should look with disfavour on stale claims and, in consequence, most legal systems provide periods of limitation within which an action must be brought once the cause of action has accrued. There are two principal methods by which this may be done: (a) by providing that, after the lapse of the stipulated time, the right on which the claim is based shall cease to exist: (b) by ruling that, though still in existence, such right shall cease to be enforceable by action

[1] See R.S.C. Order 48
[2] *Von Hellfeld v. Rechnitzer & Mayer Frères & Co.* [1914] 1 Ch. 748

after the stated period. These courses are generally described as 'barring the right' and 'barring the remedy' respectively. Both are known in English law. Under the Limitation Act 1939, rights of ownership are extinguished in land, after twelve years' adverse possession, in chattels, after six years. Hence, if B ejects A from Greenacre, A must take action to reassert his ownership within twelve years or his title will be determined: in like manner, A's goods, taken from him by B, will cease to be A's, if he delays more than six years before trying to recover them. For all other kinds of right, the Act provides that the remedy is barred after six years; i.e., it only bars the remedy, a process which was universal in English law before 1939. So, if B owes A £500 under a contract, A will be unable to sue B for the sum after six years, though still entitled to receive it. If, after seven years, B were to give the money to A, he would only be performing a duty which, in law, still rested upon him; A would have a right to the money and so, if B later regretted honouring his debt, he would not be able to recover the money again as having been paid to A, say, without consideration.

It may well be that foreign limitation provisions become relevant in an English action, e.g., if A sues B in respect of a contract governed by Utopian law and B pleads that the Utopian limitation period is four years, while A's cause of action arose five years ago. It then has to be determined whether the limitation provision is one of substance or of procedure; for, if the Utopian provision is procedural, it cannot affect proceedings in England where the rules of the *forum* will be applicable and the question will then be whether A's claim is in time by English law. The manner in which English private international law resolves this problem is the following: if the foreign limitation period provision —within its own system of law—bars the right of the plaintiff, it is a rule of substance and will be given effect in an English action, if that legal system is the law governing the dispute: if it only bars the remedy, then it is procedural and will be ignored, the timeliness of the action being then determined by English law. Thus, in our example, if the Utopian four-year period bars A's right in Utopian law, B's defence will be valid: if it only bars A's remedy, the action here will succeed, for English law will govern the matter, under which A has six years in which to sue.

These principles were enunciated by Tindal C.J. in *Huber v. Steiner*:[1] in that case, an action was brought here on a negotiable instrument made in France, after five but before six years had elapsed from the time that the note became due. The French limitation period was five years, but the action nevertheless succeeded, the French period being regarded as barring only the remedy. The fact that the Scots limitation period affected only the remedy produced a different result in *British Linen Co. v. Drummond*,[2] an action arising out of a contract governed by Scots law and made between Scots in Scotland: as it was brought more than six years after the cause of action had accrued, it failed notwithstanding that the Scots period was considerably longer.

It must be noted that, in respect of claims to immovables, the general principles adumbrated above yield to the *lex situs*: if, for whatever reason, that legal system would no longer allow the plaintiff to assert his claim, then his action in England will fail. Finally, if there be no proof of the manner in which the relevant foreign system regards its limitation provision, then it is presumed to operate in the same way as its English counterpart. Accordingly, an English court would, in the absence of evidence of the law, regard a foreign limitation provision as barring the right in claims of ownership and, in other cases, barring the remedy.

C. Evidence

As pertaining to the manner in which trial of an action is to be conducted, rules of evidence are clearly matters of procedure and therefore governed by the *lex fori*. Consequently, such questions as whether a particular witness is competent to give evidence, whether a given piece of evidence is admissible, etc., will be determined by English law.

Difficult problems of classification, however, may arise, in connection with the question of the burden of proof, by reason of the existence of presumptions. Whether it is for the plaintiff to establish, or for the defendant to disprove, a given fact is clearly —in the abstract—a matter of procedure, because it relates to the

[1] (1835) 2 Bing. N.C. 202
[2] (1830) 10 B. & C. 903

manner in which that fact is to be ascertained. Hence, the burden of proof would seem to be a procedural question. The effect of a presumption is generally to shift the burden of proof from the party on whom it would normally rest to the other. For instance, a basic rule of English evidence is that the person who asserts a fact has the duty of proving it: there is, however, also a presumption in English law that conduct is regular and lawful (*omnia rite esse acta*). Suppose that, for the purpose of an action by A against B, it is important that it be established that X was married to the woman with whom he cohabited for twenty years: the presumption arising from X's cohabitation will ensure that it is for B to establish that X was in fact not married. It would seem therefore that presumptions should also be regarded as procedural.

Presumptions, however, vary in their force. Some may be rebutted by contrary evidence while others are irrebuttable. To use English examples, the presumption of lawful conduct is rebuttable. Similarly, the presumption that a wife is entitled to pledge her husband's credit for the purchase of household necessaries can be countered by the husband's proving that the ménage was already adequately supplied with goods of the type obtained by the wife. This latter presumption, however, being based upon the cohabitation of the parties as a joint household, might not unfairly be regarded as a question of agency, a matter of substantive law, and so applicable only where English law is the proper law of the contract upon which the husband is sued.

Again there are presumptions which cannot be rebutted, e.g., that a boy under fourteen is incapable of sexual intercourse. Being irrebuttable, such presumptions really operate as substantive rules of law: what difference is there between saying, 'A boy under fourteen *must be taken to be* . . .' and, 'A boy under fourteen *is* . . .'? Uthwatt J. in fact treated such a presumption as a rule of substantive law in *Re Cohn.*[1] Two persons domiciled in Germany had died in the same air raid in London and it was essential to know which died later: for such circumstances, English law provides that the younger shall be presumed to have survived the elder,[2] while the German rule is that the parties

[1] [1945] Ch. 5
[2] Law of Property Act 1925, s. 184

shall be deemed to have died simultaneously. It was argued that, being a presumption, the English rule should be applied as being a procedural rule of the *forum*. The judge, however, held that, being irrebuttable, it was really a rule of the law of succession and thus applicable where English law governed the succession. Finding the German rule to be also irrebuttable, he held it applicable in the circumstances of the case, both successions being governed by German law as the domiciliary law of the deceased.

It is undoubtedly correct to treat irrebuttable presumptions as true rules of law and thus to find them operative only when the legal system to which they belong is the *lex causae*. Other presumptions are *prima facie* procedural as determining which party has the burden of proving a particular point. It is thought, however, that the court should always be prepared to investigate the nature of a given presumption more closely—in a word, to classify such presumptions—where, as in the case of the presumed authority of the woman to pledge her husband's credit, it is peculiar to a particular branch of law and not a presumption of general applicability. In such case, the presumption may well prove, properly regarded, a matter of substantive law and so requiring application in a case where the system of law, to which the presumption belongs, is the *lex causae*.

Again, in certain types of transaction, English statutes require that a particular kind of evidence of the transaction be produced before an action will be maintainable upon it. The commonest example is the Statute of Frauds 1677, s. 4[1] of which stipulates that no action shall be brought in respect of a specified series of contracts, unless there be a note or memorandum in writing of the contract, signed by the person against whom the agreement is set up in the action. Such provisions are treated as procedural by English courts and therefore, in an action on such a contract, even though its proper law be some system in which there is no such requirement, a written memorandum of the contract must be produced. Hence, in *Leroux v. Brown*,[2] an action in respect of a contract governed by French law failed;

[1] As now amended by the Law Reform (Enforcement of Contracts) Act 1954.

[2] (1852) 12 C. B. 801

the contract, which fell within the orbit of the Statute, had been made orally and no note of it was produced by the plaintiff. It is unfortunate that English courts have treated these requirements in so literal a fashion. Though, it is true, the Statute provides simply that no action shall be brought and not that the contract shall be a nullity, the effect of its operation is that the plaintiff is deprived of his remedy. In other matters, relating to evidence, English law has, in the century since *Leroux v. Brown*, developed more enlightened views—witness *Re Cohn*. There is, therefore, much force in the widely held view that a more liberal interpretation, based upon the realities of the situation, would find the statutory provision to be substantive in its effect and so applicable only when English law is the proper law of the contract before the court.

D. Priorities

It has long been held that, where there are competing claims against property, the disposal of which is properly before the court, determination of the order in which such claims rank for satisfaction is a matter of procedure governed by the *lex fori*. Hence, e.g., in an English bankruptcy or administration of the estate of a deceased person, English law will decide the order of priority of the claims of creditors of the estate. The reason is that this question is quite unconnected with the substantive right of each creditor, merely concerning the order in which these claims shall be met. No other course, anyhow, would be practicable. X may have a good claim against Y under a contract governed by French law and Z an equally good claim under an Italian contract. In the event of Y's English bankruptcy, could an English court defensibly adopt any other order of priority than its own? Similarly, the order of claims under the law maritime against a ship is regulated by the *lex fori*. In *The Colorado*,[1] a ship had been mortgaged to a Frenchman and was also subject to a claim by a firm of English ship repairers for repairs executed. In French law, the repairers' claim would have ranked before that of the mortgagee, but in English law the order is reversed. The Court of Appeal accordingly held that the Frenchman had priority over the English ship repairers.

[1] [1923] P. 103

E. REMEDIES

Whatever the law which governs the right of the plaintiff, the remedy to which he is entitled in England will be determined by English law. Provided that, under the appropriate *lex causae*, a person has a good claim, then he may receive in an English court any remedy which is available in England for the protection of the type of right that he asserts. Thus in *Baschet v. London Illustrated Standard*,[1] a French publisher was held entitled, under the International Copyright Act 1886, to an injunction against the defendants, an English company which had pirated some of his pictures, although that remedy would not be forthcoming by French law, under which his copyright arose.

In like manner, it will be for English law to decide whether a set-off may be allowed in an English action. Suppose that A sues B in England for a debt of £500, A himself being indebted to B for £300: English law determines whether B can set off this £300 against A's claim, so reducing it in effect to a claim for £200: *Meyer v. Dresser*.[2] The reason for this perfectly proper rule is that questions of set-off are procedural in that they determine whether one action is sufficient to adjust the rights of the parties or whether each party must assert his right in a separate action.

The commonest of remedies is, of course, damages, a money award the object of which is, in general, to compensate the plaintiff for the loss which he has suffered as a result of the breach of right complained off—to put him in the position in which he would have been without the infraction of that right. That statement, however, needs some qualification.

In English law itself, a plaintiff does not necessarily recover damages representing the monetary equivalent of all the loss he has in fact suffered. In the law of contract, for instance, the principle is essentially that a defendant will be liable to make compensation for such damage as a reasonable man might be presumed, at the making of the contract, to have foreseen as the probable result of its breach.[3] Suppose that A agrees to sell a

[1] (1900) 69 L.J.Ch. 35
[2] (1864) 16 C.B.N.S. 646
[3] See *Hadley v. Baxendale* (1854) 9 Ex. 341: *Victoria Laundry v. Newman* [1948] 2 All E.R. 806

car to B for £300 and that B has an agreement with C to sell the car to C for £500: if A in breach of contract fails to deliver the car to B, the latter will lose the £200 profit that would have accrued from the resale to C. But in an action against A, B would not necessarily receive damages in respect of that loss of profit. If A and B were simply two ordinary individuals, A might foresee that the loss which B would sufferfrom his failure to deliver the car would be that B would not have the vehicle on the due date and thus would be deprived of its value then. But, if A had performed the obligation resting on him, B would have had to pay him £300. Accordingly, the loss that A must foresee as ensuing upon a breach of contract is the difference between the value of the car on the date when delivery should have been made (for which, one normally takes the market value of such a car) and £300; that is the minimum liability which could rest on A. Hence, if such a car would cost £400 on the open market, then B can recover £100 damages from A.

If, on the other hand, A knew that B was a secondhand car dealer and was buying this car for the purpose of his business, then he could reasonably be held to foresee a possibility of loss to B in respect of a resale—even though A did not know of the particular agreement with C—if he himself failed to deliver the car. Thus B would be entitled to some amount (not necessarily £200) to represent his loss of profit. Again, if B told A that he had the sub-contract with C for immediate resale, then A, knowing the full facts of the situation, would be liable for the full loss of profit, £200. In the law of tort, again, actual loss and actionable loss are not of necessity synonymous.[1]

In fact, the same principle—that actual loss is not always recoverable—is to be found throughout the law. The general statement of principle, therefore, concerning damages must be reformulated somewhat as follows: The object of damages is to put the party injured, so far as money will do it, in the position in which he would have been, in the eyes of the law, if the defendant had complied with his duty. That is the legal extent of compensation by way of damages.

The matters here referred to are generally designated

[1] cf. *Re Polemis & Furness Withy and Co.* [1921] 3 K.B. 560 and *Edison v. Liesboch* [1933] A.C. 449

compendiously the problem of measure of damages. But in truth, as Professor Cheshire pointed out,[1] two questions really arise. The fact that all actual loss may not be recoverable raises first a question as to the extent of the liability of the defendant: for how much of the loss which he has in fact occasioned to the plaintiff can he in law be held liable? This is the question of remoteness of damage—loss which may not be claimed for by the plaintiff is 'too remote' from the defendant's conduct to be properly chargeable to him. Only when this question has been determined does it become necessary to translate the loss so found actionable into terms of money; and that is when the question of measure of damages really arises.

Being a question of the extent of liability, the matter of remoteness of damage is one of substance; it is the determination of the question, What is the liability of the defendant? Hence it should be resolved by the *lex causae* in a private international law case. Only the value to be set upon the liability determined by the *lex causae* should be regarded as a question of remedy and, as such, of procedure to be answered by the *lex fori*.

For this view that the *lex causae* determines the extent of liability, there is now English authority in *D'Almeida Aruajo Ltd. v. Sir Frederick Becker & Co., Ltd.*[2] A had agreed, by a contract governed by Portuguese law, to sell 500 tons of palm oil to B. Because of B's breach of contract, A committed a breach of agreement with C, for which A had to pay C an indemnity. In an action by A against B, the question now arose whether A could recover the amount of this indemnity as damages for B's breach of contract. Pilcher J. held that this was a question of liability and therefore was governed by Portuguese law as the proper law of the A/B contract. In tort, the principle is, perhaps, less important because, as seen, the action as constituted before an English court is an English action in respect of an English tort. Consequently, English law governs both the question of liability and the monetary assessment thereof, provided that the conduct of the defendant was 'not justifiable' by the *lex loci delicti*. Thus in *Kohnke v. Karger*,[3] further damages were awarded

[1] See Cheshire, *Private International Law* (4th ed.) p. 659
[2] [1953] 2 Q.B. 329
[3] [1951] 2 All E.R. 179

to the plaintiff in respect of injuries suffered in a motor accident in France, despite the fact that she had received some in proceedings in France, because the French court had not taken account of all the legally recoverable loss.

Once the *lex causae* has determined the extent of liability, however, the assessment thereof by the adjudicating court is entirely a matter of remedy and so governed by the *lex fori*. Hence, English standards of assessment will apply in an action in England, although the law governing the dispute be some foreign system. Such assessment is a translation into terms of actual money of the recoverable loss: in the illustration used earlier, for instance, reference to the market value of the car and to the sum agreed by the parties would give the court criteria by which to fix the money value of the plaintiff's loss.

It may well be, especially when the *lex causae* of a case is a foreign legal system, that ideally such assessment should be made in terms of some foreign currency, e.g., in francs to quantify the damages due in respect of breach of a contract governed by French law. An English order may be made, however, only in terms of sterling.

Consequently, problems of conversion arise; and, since the exchange rate of currencies may fluctuate, the court must have a guide to the rate of exchange upon which to base its conversion into sterling when giving judgment in such an action. The English rule is that the rate prevailing at the time that the loss in question was incurred shall be taken. Thus in *S.S. Celia v. S.S. Volturno*,[1] after a collision between an English and an Italian ship, the Italian vessel was detained for repairs: the House of Lords held that its owners' claim, made in terms of lire, for the period of such detention should be converted into sterling on the basis of the exchange rate operative when the detention occurred. More recently, in *Cummings v. London Bullion Co.*,[2] an American had bought a brooch from the defendants for $3,200 on the understanding that it might be returned and the money refunded. Some time later, the buyer decided to return the brooch. Before the money could be refunded, the consent of the Treasury to the transfer of dollars was necessary and, by the time that such

[1] [1921] 2 A.C. 544
[2] [1952] 1 K.B. 327

consent had been obtained, the pound was devalued in relation to the U.S. dollar. In this action by the American for the refund of the money, the question was the rate of exchange on which the amount payable to the defendants was to be assessed. The Court of Appeal held that, as the promise of repayment could not lawfully be honoured until the Treasury authorized the payment, the rate prevailing when that permission was given governed the question. The defendants thus had to pay a much greater sum in sterling than would have been the case when the contract was made or, indeed, when the brooch was actually returned.

INDEX

www.ingramcontent.com/pod-product-compliance
Ingram Content Group UK Ltd.
Pitfield, Milton Keynes, MK11 3LW, UK
UKHW020207290926
15470UKWH00001B/48

9 780837 17929